WITHDRAWN

HARVARD LIBRARY

WITHDRAWN

THE INTERPRETIVE ROLE OF THE RELIGIOUS COMMUNITY IN FRIEDRICH SCHLEIERMACHER AND JOSIAH ROYCE

HEAVENLY BONDS

THE INTERPRETIVE ROLE OF THE RELIGIOUS COMMUNITY IN FRIEDRICH SCHLEIERMACHER AND JOSIAH ROYCE
HEAVENLY BONDS

Gayle D. Beebe

The Edwin Mellen Press
Lewiston•Queenston•Lampeter

BL
53
.B364
1999

Library of Congress Cataloging-in-Publication Data

Beebe, Gayle D.
   The interpretive role of the religious community in Friedrich
Schleiermacher and Josiah Royce : heavenly bonds / Gayle D. Beebe.
     p.   cm.
   Includes bibliographical references and index.
   ISBN 0-7734-1977-2
   1. Experience (Religion) 2. Christian communities.
3. Schleiermacher, Friedrich, 1768-1834. 4. Royce, Josiah,
1855-1916. I. Title. II. Title: Heavenly bonds.
   BL53.B364   1999
   291.6' 5--dc21   98-43822
                                    CIP

A CIP catalog record for this book is available from the British Library.

Copyright © 1999 Gayle D. Beebe

All rights reserved. For information contact

The Edwin Mellen Press   The Edwin Mellen Press
Box 450   Box 67
Lewiston, New York   Queenston, Ontario
USA 14092-0450   CANADA L0S 1L0

The Edwin Mellen Press, Ltd.
Lampeter, Ceredigion, Wales
UNITED KINGDOM SA48 8LT

Printed in the United States of America

8/02/11 Mellon 225872

Dedication

This book is dedicated to the people who matter the most to me and who are often on my heart when my head must attend to other matters:

My wife,	Pamela;
My daughters,	Anna Nicole and Elizabeth Marie;
Our parents,	Dennis and Janet Hagen,
	Norma Beebe and the memory of my father,
	Richard Beebe;

And our immediate families.

Thank you for your love, prayer, encouragement and support.

Contents

FOREWARD   ix

Chapter 1. Introduction   1
    The Nature of the Problem   1
    Overview and Approach   5

I. THE NATURE OF INTERPRETATION IN SCHLIERMACHER AND ROYCE

Chapter 2.   The Nature of Interpretation in Schleiermacher   9
    The Nature of Grammatical and Technical Interpretation   10
    The Role of Tradition in Interpretation   12
    Criticisms and Clarification   14
    The Importance of Oral and Written Forms of Language Use   17

Chapter 3.   The Nature of Interpretation in Royce   22

    Coherence and Contingency in Royce's Theory of Interpretation   22
    The Role of Signs in the Process of Interpretation   31
    The One Event   32
    The Founder of Christianity   34

II. THE NATURE OF THE COMMUNITY IN SCHLEIRMACHER AND ROYCE

Chapter 4.   The Nature of the Religious Community in Schleiermacher   39

    The Nature and Function of the Religious Community
        in the Speeches   40
    Individual Religious Experience and the Need
        for Religious Community   47
    The Development of Religious Consciousness through Particular
        Religious Communities   50
    Why Religious Communities Differ   52
    The Religious Use of Language   54
    The Influence of Jesus   55
    The Role of Preaching   58

The Role of the Holy Spirit/Common Spirit 60
The Role of Doctrines in the Formation of
      Christian Religious Consciousness 65
The Role of Tradition and Scripture 69

Chapter 5.   The Religious Nature of the Community in Royce 75

The Overarching Concerns 75
The Sources of Religious Insight 79
Social Nature Realized in Communities 84
The Role of Hope and Memory 87
The Metaphysical Foundation of Religious Experience 90
The Individual and the Collective 92
The Nature of Communities 97
The Religious Nature of the True Community 99
The Role of the Will 101
The Universal and the Particular and the
      Development of a New Consciousness 104
Love as Loyalty 108
Contemporary Discussions Concerning the Role of the Religious
      Community as Anticipated by Royce 109

III. THE INTERPRETIVE ROLE OF THE RELIGIOUS COMMUNITY
     IN SCHLEIERMACHER AND ROYCE

Chapter 6. The Interpretive Role of the Religious Community
           in Schleiermacher 116

The Role of Piety 116
The Role of the Religious and Sensible Self-Consciousness 118
The Role of the Essential Features of the Church 122
The Role of Scripture 124
The Role of Preaching 126
The Role of the Sacraments 127
Baptism 128
The Lord's Supper 129
The Role of Prayer 130
The Role of Christian Worship 131
The Coherence Producing Role of the Church 132
The Role of the Church in the World 133

Chapter 7.   The Religious Nature of Communities of
                          Interpretation in Royce   139

         The Interpretive Role of the Religious Community
                  in the Formation of Religious Consciousness   141
         The Universal Element of Communal Consciousness   146
         The Role of the Will   152
         The Moral Burden Which Awakens Human Consciousness   155
         The Nature of Salvation   157
         Integrative Insight of Schleiermacher and Royce   161

Chapter 8. Concluding Thoughts   169

         Postscript: Issues for Further Research   174

         Selected Bibliography   178

         Index   190

FOREWORD

The thought of Friedrich Schleiermacher has so often been represented in passing discussions in terms of his view of religious apprehension whether by means of the intuition and feeling of the divine or the immediate self-consciousness of utter dependence that other important aspects of his theology and philosophy have remained in the shadows. Certainly one aspect of such neglect is Schleiermacher's concern with the nature and dynamics of religious community. In the Speeches, for instance, the importance of association in religion is fundamental to the movement of the work, but its contribution as focused in the fourth speech is too rarely explored.

Gayle Beebe in this book has brought Schleiermacher's thinking on religious community into the light and shows how the religious knowing of the individual has its setting and formation in a community. Schleiermacher's profound appreciation of the social formation of religion is given prominence by showing its relation to the thought of the "American philosopher, Josiah Royce, formulated at the beginning of the twentieth century. Sociality was important for virtually all of Royce's work throughout his career, but after 1900 Royce turned the emphasis of his reflection to the exploration of more concrete experience in several ways, and especially in religious and Christian themes. It is this more experientially oriented Royce that Beebe finds to be so pertinent to juxtapose to Schleiermacher on Christianity and community.

One highly important and intriguing aspect of the overlapping communal concerns of these two thinkers is found in their creative approach to the issue of interpretation. Schleiermacher has found increasing recognition of his seminal role in the emergence of the modern philosophy of hermeneutics. He insisted that this disciplined investigation of the meaning manifested in the language of documents from the past derived its principles from the process of understanding another person in community. Schleiermacher's own reflection on this subject took place in close alliance with the interpreting of the New Testament.

On his part, Royce came in his post 1900 philosophy to a theory of interpretation based upon the historical nature of a community and the movement of time. In The Problem of Christianity these and kindred issues became focused for Royce through his consideration of the role of the writings of Paul in the New

Testament. Paul is viewed by Royce as "the interpreter" who takes the words and actions of Jesus of Nazareth and concretizes their meaning for the community in a new situation. Royce holds that this means that Christianity involves not only a way of life but also an ontological manifestation of "the real world."

Gayle Beebe's analysis of Schleiermacher and Royce elucidates both the overlap and commonality of their thought on religion and community, and the mutual enrichment which they offer the views of each other. Schleiermacher's community is more firmly rooted and vivified by its historical base in Christian origins. On the other hand, Royce brings out more forcibly the task produced by the claims of a new situation for the Christian church and the new community that can result when the task is creatively accomplished. With Beebe's guidance this is a very fruitful interaction of the resources of Schleiermacher and Royce.

Jack Verheyden
Claremont Graduate University

Chapter 1

Introduction

The Nature of the Problem

The thesis of this project is that all modern attempts to elevate individual religious experience above and separate from contextualization in the religious community are impoverished. It is not, 'I think, therefore, I am,' but, 'we are, therefore, I am.' Religious communities and individual religious experiences are inextricably linked; one cannot be had without the other. Of specific interest is the way in which religious communities provide the context within which religious experiences can be interpreted and understood. At the heart of this project is a recognition that if humans are incurably religious, then they appear to be unequally affected by religion. Religious consciousness develops in specific ways. It is historical and time-bound. It is influenced by language, culture and community. By utilizing the work of Friedrich Schleiermacher and Josiah Royce, the primary role of the religious community in the interpretation of religious experience will be demonstrated.

In considering the interpretive role of the religious community it is essential that a working definition of religious experience is established. The many attempts to define religious experience are as varied as they are complex. The word often used to define religious experience, mysticism, is a derivative of the Greek term, 'muein,' which means to remain silent.[1] Originally, it pertained specifically to the Greek Mystery Religions and included the acquisition of special knowledge leading to mystical insight. As early as 1899, W. R. Inge offered as many as 26 different definitions of mysticism in an appendix to his definitive work, but summarized his study by suggesting that, "...true mysticism is the attempt to realize, in thought and feeling, the immanence of the temporal in the eternal, and of the eternal in the temporal."[2] Evelyn Underhill, writing twelve years later suggested that mysticism is the "expression of the innate tendency of

---

[1] Louis Dupre, "Mysticism," p. 245, <u>Encyclopedia of Religion, vol. #10.</u> Edited by Mircea Eliade (New York: MacMillan Pub. Company, 1987).
[2] Inge, William Ralph. <u>Christian Mysticism.</u> (London: Methuen Publishing Company, 1899), p. 335.

the human heart towards complete harmony with the transcendental order...”[3]
Ernst Troeltsch, writing a year later, extended this definition by identifying
mysticism as the primacy of direct or immediate religious experience.[4]   Rufus
Jones, a contemporary and friend of Josiah Royce, defined mysticism as,

> the type of religion which puts the emphasis on
> immediate awareness of relation with God, on
> direct and intimate consciousness of the Divine
> presence. It is religion in its most acute, intense,
> and living stage.[5]

The unanswered question in all of these definitions of religious experience
is: Why do human beings have specific experiences which they interpret
religiously and what role does the religious community play in mediating the
meaning which these experiences provide? As Schleiermacher and Royce attest,
religious experience occurs as an individual opens to an ultimate center of value
that provides meaning in life. All aspects of humanity's historical existence are
potential bridges to this center of ultimate value. In order to get there, however,
one needs contact with an overarching ideal contextualized in a community and
mediated through interpretation.

A lingering problem with this understanding continues, however, as
contemporary efforts to promote a 'religionless religion' have impoverished
attempts to understand the role the religious community plays in interpreting
religious experience. The term, 'religionless religion,' has gained currency in
recent times by suggesting that the role of the religious community in matters
religious must decrease while the role of the individual, and of the individual's
religious quest, independent of all religious communities, must increase.[6]

On the surface, it appears this emphasis on individualism and independent

---

[3] Underhill, Evelyn. Mysticism. (New York: Doubleday, 1911; reprinted in 1990).
[4] Troeltsch, Ernst. The Social Teaching of the Christian Churches, Vol. I,II. (Lousiville,
KY: Westminster/John Know Press, 1992); originally published in German in 1912 and
translated into English in 1931 by George Allen and Unwin Ltd., London and the
Macmillan Co., New York.
[5] Jones, Rufus. Studies in Mystical Religion. (New York: MacMillan and Co., Ltd., 1923),
p. xv.
[6] John Hick, "Exaugural Address," School of Theology at Claremont, published by the
Department of Religion, Claremont Graduate School, May, 1992.

inquiry is correct. The emergence of interest in a common core to religious experience, independent of and elevated above all religious traditions and communities, has accentuated the need for the individual to pursue religious understanding on his or her own. While this trend has accelerated in recent years, it gained its original momentum from Rene Descartes and reached its apex in Europe with Immanuel Kant and in America with William James.

In Schleiermacher's time, Immanuel Kant launched a new direction in religious inquiry when he defended limiting reason to make room for faith. By limiting reason, Kant believed he could render belief in God reliable and the authority of morality essential by demonstrating that although one is unable to apprehend God through pure reason, the mind still has an idea of God which it did not create and which only becomes meaningful by association with a particular domain of one's experience.

The logic behind Kant's argument is as follows: first, all knowledge is based on experience, but all knowledge does not arise from experience. Second, experiences occur in succession. Third, to experience anything one must have a unity of experience. Fourth, a unity of experience implies a unity of self. Fifth, a unity of self is as much a product of experience as anything else. Sixth, to have an experience of a unity of self implies synthesizing acts which precede this experience. And finally, these synthesizing acts are the categories which Kant locates in the transcendental unity of apperception.

This logic is Kant's way of rendering the possibility of knowing anything external to oneself without digressing into either the pure rationalism of Descartes or the radical empiricism of Locke. Kant did not imagine that it was possible to know a thing-in-itself, but equally powerful was his conviction that one could experience the thing and not just some idea of it. The synthesizing activity of the transcendental unity of apperception allows this knowledge to come forth because it is the nature and operation of the human self to order his or her world in accordance with these universal categories.

By introducing the concept that though humanity wants to believe in certain ideas that go beyond the domain of reason, there is equally valid evidence to undermine this belief (the Antinomies), Kant believed he was doing religious faith a favor by showing that the idea of God was not, in fact, vulnerable to counter arguments which sought to disprove God's existence. By separating reason from faith, Kant argued that reason operates on the basis of facts ascertainable through scientific logic, whereas faith operates on the basis of value ascertainable through practical reason. God, freedom and immortality are three ideas which cannot be accounted for on the basis of experience alone. From whence then do they arise? This question led Kant to establish his theory of practical reason as the domain of value and morality.

By insisting on this limitation of reason in order to make room for faith, Kant also insisted on the necessity of freedom in order to make obligation necessary. If there was not infinite freedom for the human, then the necessary desire for obligation could not be required. This emphasis on freedom and obligation tried to move beyond the mere environmental determinism of Locke and the random benevolence of Hume by grounding morality in the freedom of the will to align itself with obligation. Thus, the culmination of Kant's project was to retain the individual as the first and primary arbiter of meaning and value. Kant certainly never resolved this issue fully, but his articulation of the problem and the inroads he made in answering the question were more instrumental in forming the framework within which Schleiermacher responded then any other single thinker.[7]

In Royce's time, William James' The Varieties of Religious Experiences, made a similar impact. Arguing for a common core to individual religious experience, James outlined a definition of religious experience which identified four common elements found in all religious experience: ineffability, noetic, transiency, and passivity.[8]

Ineffability is essential to religious experience and expresses the inability of language and concept to articulate this state or experience adequately.[9] A noetic quality is also an essential ingredient in defining religious experience and is

---

[7] Kant, Immanuel. Religion Within the Limits of Reason Alone. Originally published in 1793. Translated by Theodore M. Greene and Hoyt H. Hudson. (San Francisco: Harper and Row, 1934, 1960).
[8] James, William. The Varieties of Religious Experience. New York: Mentor Books, 1958 edition, originally published in 1901, pp. 292-293.
[9] James, William. Ibid.

defined by its ability to enlarge one's perspective, alter one's conscious awareness, or, in some way, shift a person's outlook from one point of view to another.[10] Transiency is a third element of mystical experience and is not essential. When one describes a religious experience it often seems present as a state that comes and goes but does not endure.[11] Passivity, the fourth quality, suggests that the individual does not produce the religious experience, but can, through certain disciplines, prepare for it.[12]

The impact of James' work is impossible to underestimate. Of critical significance is the effect his focus on the individual nature of religious experience has had in diminishing the role and importance of religious communities and traditions. Although James illuminated a vital part of the religious life in his emphasis on individual religious experience, he did so by diminishing the importance of the religious community whose influence and impact often preceded and shaped such individual experiences.[13] Because of James' insistence on individual religious experience, the theological and doctrinal dimensions of the religious community were often diminished and frequently ignored.

Overview and Approach

The purpose of this dissertation is to demonstrate the way in which Royce and Schleiermacher respond to the rise of Enlightenment individualism and the diminishment of the role of the religious community to secondary status in one's understanding of religion and religious experience. This project is divided into three sections each of which begins with Schleiermacher's insights and then

---

[10] James, William. Ibid., p. 293. John Hick discusses this sort of change or transformation as a change from self-centeredness to reality-centeredness. See An Interpretation of Religion. New Haven: Yale University Press, 1989.

[11] James, Wm. Ibid.

[12] James, Wm. Ibid. Bertrand Russell, in, Mysticism and Logic and Other Essays, notes four areas he considers typical of mystical experience. First, insights based on intuition take precedence over reason, sense and analysis. Reality, therefore, lies behind the world of appearance. Second, all reality is unified. Third, the temporal dimension of reality is denied. And fourth, all evil is mere appearance. Besides failing to offer cogent examples that substantiate his thesis, Russell also ignores the possibility of an experience interpreted mystically which reorders one's understanding and life and leads one to enter into a religious community.

[13] James, Wm. Ibid., p. 31.

concludes with Royce's extension of these insights. Where Schleiermacher is weak, Royce is strong and where Royce is weak, Schleiermacher is strong. Schleiermacher excels, for example, at demonstrating the way in which particular religious communities form. But Royce excels at extending Schleiermacher's consideration of the religious community to demonstrate the religious nature of all true communities. By integrating their thought a compelling argument is offered which addresses the fundamental challenge both Schleiermacher and Royce confront: how can one make sense of contingent experiences without relating these experiences to an ultimate unifying ideal which resides in the religious community?

In attempting to answer this dilemma consideration will begin with the way in which interpretation acts to produce human understanding. Four concerns are particularly critical. First, it will be necessary to show why one must move beyond the endless oscillation of twin foci as identified by Schleiermacher to embrace Royce's theory of triadic interpretation. Next, the way in which language use builds bridges will be noted. Then, the way in which communities contextualize language use will help define the way in which interpretation, anchored to community, can produce the unifying ideals which mediate salvation. Finally, the way in which Schleiermacher and Royce both recognize the potential of every contingent experience to mediate an ultimate reality will be noted. Of particular interest is the way in which individual religious experience must be interpreted in the broader context of community if the experience is to carry meaning and help mediate one's 'salvation.'

These concerns capture the essence of the religious quest and reflect the spirit necessary to find an ultimate unifying ideal. As individual religious experience is contextualized within the community, moreover, it will become evident that what is dominant in religion, as with all of life, is not the individual experience, but the meaning derived from the experience through the interpretive role of the community. In this way, the manner by which a community structures individual interpretation and understanding will be demonstrated. What Royce, in particular, is anxious to demonstrate is since the human is always acting and interpreting, how does the human act and interpret in relation to a higher ideal.

In Section II, the way in which communities form around shared understandings will be identified. Communities provide structure for human contingencies. A community embodies a particular way of seeing the world and reflects how contingent experiences can relate to an overarching ideal. Communities, moreover, provide the context in which signs and symbols are appropriated, reviewed, rejected or embraced based on their ability to make sense of individual experiences. Communities are not individuals, but as Royce will demonstrate, they can be organized around an ultimate center of meaning and value. Communities are not the ultimate center of meaning and value, but communities can witness to that center and can be organized by people who recognize that center.

Additionally, communities are preserved by doctrines and traditions. The difference which Schleiermacher and Royce both highlight between genuine or true communities and common communities is the fact that genuine communities are formed from spiritual acts of the will whereas common communities cluster around natural characteristics and parochial concerns.

Communities form, as Schleiermacher and Royce note, as a reflection of the fundamental nature of reality. By utilizing Schleiermacher and Royce, the way in which different communities provide different unifying ideals can be demonstrated. A community's ideal gains preeminence as a result of its ability to remain plausible as the best unifying explanation of contingent reality. By considering the nature of particular communities the manner in which the realm of human contingency connects with the realm of ultimate ideals can be demonstrated. An inherent danger with this thesis, however, is the fact that historical realities, which are meant to create bonds with ultimate ideals, can become substitutes for the actual ideals. Nevertheless, it is the responsibility of the temporal community to teach its members how to look beyond the contingent domain to the unifying domain where ultimate ideals reside in the 'Beloved Community.'

Since communities contextualize the way in which language can be used such language use activities as preaching, doctrine, tradition, and scripture all reflect particular understandings contextualized within community. By expanding

Schleiermacher's treatment of the religious use of language, moreover, Royce will demonstrate the way in which words can build bridges between particular experiences and ultimate ideals. In this way, Royce will demonstrate the way in which every aspect of human experience, including suffering and death, can be signs which mediate meaning when interpreted.

In Section III, the way in which religious communities (Schleiermacher) and the religious nature of all true communities (Royce) are fused will demonstrate the manner in which the context of interpretation is constituted. In this context, interpretation functions within community to establish and strengthen the unifying bonds between individual experiences and ultimate ideals. These interpretations of individual experiences, which mediate salvation, are anchored to the community and help to generate and sustain particular forms of communal consciousness. Thus, such activities as preaching, baptism, communion and prayer are individual activities which can carry a deeper meaning by producing contact with an ultimate unifying ideal.

In extending Schleiermacher's treatment of particular communities, Royce will show the necessity of establishing communities that not only embody an ideal, but pattern human life in such a way that humans can attend to this ideal. Traditions and doctrines, for example, create contact with a shared past which gives meaning and understanding to a present community. In this way, the ideals distilled in the history, traditions, and doctrines of a particular community become not the ideal itself, but a bridge to the ideal. As such, ideals tied to history, tradition, and doctrine are contingent, but they can mediate ultimate meaning when used properly.

In the pages that follow it will be demonstrated that neither Schleiermacher nor Royce want to change the way religious communities are constituted; they want to change the way communities act upon their members in their role as the mediator of ultimate ideals. In fulfilling this task, it is hoped that recognition of the reality that humans are not unencumbered selves, but historical, social, and cultural bound beings will be realized.

Section I. The Nature of Interpretation in Schleiermacher and Royce

Chapter Two

The Nature of Interpretation in Schleiermacher

In seeking to understand the interpretive role of the religious community in Schleiermacher it is necessary to begin with his theory of hermeneutics which underlies all human understanding. For Schleiermacher, hermeneutics, at its best, is the attempt by two or more people to understand one another through language. To accomplish this task, Schleiermacher advocates that understanding through language involves four significant processes.

First, to understand language and its use one must see it in terms of the actions and intentions of the speaker. Second, these actions and intentions of the speaker only make sense when the context in which they were communicated is grasped.[14] That is, words and phrases make sense only when situated within a context. Third, these actions and intentions, situated in a particular context of communication, reveal both a language and a person. In other words, we come to understand language use and the nature of a person through their actions and intentions manifested in language. Since people anticipate a certain level of understanding by their audience, then one must assume that the audience understood it.[15]   And fourth, understanding, which is the final goal of hermeneutics, occurs when it is clear why a person or persons used language in the specific way in which they did, based on the community or communal context to which they addressed themselves.[16]

---

[14] Schleiermacher, Friedrich. Hermeneutics: The Handwritten Manuscripts. Edited by Heinz Kimmerle. Translated by James Duke and Jack Forstman. Missoula, MT: Scholars Press, 1977, p. 43.

[15] Schleiermacher, F. Ibid., p. 58.

[16] Schleiermacher, F. Ibid., pp. 97-98.

The Nature of Grammatical and Technical Interpretation

In addressing these four claims, Schleiermacher separates his treatment of hermeneutics into grammatical interpretation and technical interpretation. Grammatical interpretation is concerned with how language is used; technical interpretation is concerned with what we learn of a person through his or her use of language. Grammatical interpretation attempts to determine meaning from the context and to locate the sphere within which specific uses of language have meaning.[17]

Schleiermacher's point is to try to show that language and its uses reflect a specific consciousness fastened to and embedded within a particular community. As such, language, and the people who use it, have a reciprocal influence on each other. Language shapes one's consciousness while the specific ways in which one expresses one's consciousness shapes language.[18]   Thus, to use a language properly, one must be familiar with the way(s) in which language is used within a specific community.[19]

Thus, language serves a primary purpose of binding the lives of people together in community.[20]   Schleiermacher amplifies this point by stating,

> ...the interpreter must be familiar with the whole sphere of life and the relationships between author and audience since these reflect a specific communal consciousness."[21]

Earlier, Schleiermacher had introduced the idea of 'sphere' by referring to the necessity of understanding anything in part by its relation to the whole.[22]   In defining specific spheres, moreover, Schleiermacher laid the groundwork for

---

[17] Ibid., p. 117, 127.

[18] Schleiermacher, F. Ibid., p. 99.

[19] This is similar to a point made by Wittgenstein as treated by John Murphy in his unpublished doctoral dissertation, Mysticism and Epistemology: A Study and Comparison of Modern Philosophical Analyses of Mysticism and the Thought of Ludwig Wittgenstein. Claremont Graduate School, Claremont, CA, 1995.

[20] Schleiermacher, F. Ibid., p. 204.

[21] Schleiermacher, F. Ibid., p. 216.

[22] Schleiermacher, F. Ibid., p. 60.

introducing the religious use of language within the context of the religious community and, in turn, the development of specific interpretations of religious experience mediated by the use of language in a religious community.

What Schleiermacher is suggesting is the reality language, as a revealer of the self, contains more than merely the resources of the self. In his efforts to recognize the broader impacts of the community, Schleiermacher also recognizes the broader context of language-use within the community. When a self uses language and another self understands, it is the words used between the individuals which build community. The understanding of these words through interpretation provides meaning. Thus, Schleiermacher is concerned with how words form particular connections between people, that, when interpreted, form a community of understanding that provides meaning.

A mistake frequently made in dealing with Schleiermacher's theory of interpretation is to focus exclusively on his lectures on hermeneutics without placing these lectures in the broader perspective of his understanding of the religious community. For example, in the Christian Faith, Schleiermacher articulates the way in which the Christian church represents a particular form of a religious community. As a community, it reflects certain understandings of social theory which he considers in his treatment of philosophical ethics. As a religious community, it contains a distinct form of religious piety which is cultivated and sustained within religious communities. As a particular religious community, it reflects a specific understanding of the religious consciousness in which all aspects of the community and all aspects of the religious consciousness are related to the redemption accomplished by Jesus of Nazareth.[23] Thus, the role of the community, as the locus of interpretation, is both to preserve a distinct understanding of an ultimate life sustaining ideal and to transmit this ideal to each individual.

Within these spheres, defined as religious communities, several different speech activities occur which sustain this understanding. Sermons, creedal confessions, passing the peace, the selection and choice of hymns, and the singing of spiritual songs all reflect a particular form of communal religious

---

[23] Schleiermacher, F. Ibid., p. 52, prop. 11.

consciousness. In the process of this preservation, moreover, traditions develop which transmit these speech activities and bind the community together to form the bonds by which one can understand one's religious experiences. Schleiermacher makes a passing reference to a "common heritage" which a speaker and a hearer must have if understanding is to occur, but he does not elaborate on it or develop this idea further.[24] What it suggests, however, is precisely what is found in his treatment of spheres and that is meaning is derived within the community not from within oneself.

In the Soliloquies, Schleiermacher argued that every individual consciousness is shaped by a combination of one's personal actions and the meaning given these actions by one's group identity.[25] The community distills corporate understandings of unifying, ultimate ideals. These sustain people. To ignore these ideals is to threaten the loss of contact with the interpretive process which provides meaning. Through this influence, Schleiermacher began to identify the role religious traditions play in providing a bridge between one's individual needs and the ultimate solution to these needs in a unifying ideal.

The Role of Tradition in Interpretation

The role played by religious traditions, moreover, is akin to the role played by political traditions in shaping individual political consciousnesses. "To effectively rule," for example, Schleiermacher believed, "...one must have both effective leadership skills and be in touch with the historical traditions of the people."[26] Likewise in the religious community. Why? Because historical traditions place individuals in contact with a realm they do not normally perceive.

Schleiermacher further observed that whereas language and culture unite people, only time and tradition can produce a unified community. Traditions help shape the ongoing external expression of religion. As they are expressed, they

---

[24] Schleiermacher, F. Hermeneutics, p. 70.

[25] Schleiermacher, F. Soliloquies, pp. 121-126.

[26] Schleiermacher, F. Saematliche Werke, Zur Philosophie, II, p. 249. Jerry Dawson draws attention to this dynamic in his consideration of Schleiermacher as a patriot. See, Dawson, Jerry F. Friedrich Schleiermacher: The Evolution of a Nationalist. Austin, TX: University of Texas Press, 1966, p. 128.

establish the context in which internal states can come in contact with overarching religious ideals. Together, the external expression and the internal state typify the ideal of a community interpreting individual religious experiences in and through their unifying ideals.[27]

The trouble with traditions, however, is the individuals frequently become more interested in the traditions than the reality they distill.[28] But traditions cannot be discarded without peril. Traditions give rise to doctrine, and doctrine both shapes and reflects a particular form of religious understanding.

One must recognize the role of tradition and doctrine without elevating either to ultimate status. Nevertheless, no tradition or doctrine is without need of possible reform. Every tradition and doctrine must remain pliable in order to adjust to the changes necessitated when their apparent explanation of religious reality no longer makes sense or provides meaning.

Traditions are particularly important within the Christian scheme because it is through traditions that one can experience contact with the living spirit of Jesus Christ.[29] Thus, through traditions, this contact with Jesus Christ makes it possible to transcend one's historical contingency to find the realm of one's ultimate ideals.[30]

Traditions, thus, help establish the communal context within which Schleiermacher's idea of the hermeneutical circle can function. The hermeneutical circle reflects the establishment of a community of interpretation which gives rise to a particular form of individual and communal consciousness. Schleiermacher amplifies this point in his second address (1829) to the Berlin Academy of Sciences. In it, he identifies the way in which the whole is understood from the parts and the parts can be understood only from the whole.[31]

---

[27] Elsewhere, Schleiermacher distinguished the subordinate role of tradition in relation to Scripture. In articulating his position, Schleiermacher wrote that tradition would not be placed beside Scripture and by implication implied that it would have a subordinate role in the transmission of Christian faith.

[28] Schleiermacher, F. The Christian Faith. p. 698.

[29] Schleiermacher, F. Ibid., p. 427.

[30] Ibid., p. 588.

[31] Schleiermacher, F., "The Academy Addresses of 1829: On the Concept of Hermeneutics, with Reference to F. A. Wolf's Instructions and Ast's Textbook," Translated and Introduced by David E. Klemm, Hermeneutical Inquiry: Vol. I: The Interpretation of Texts. Atlanta, GA: Scholars Press, 1986, pp. 61-88.

Schleiermacher writes,

> The hermeneutical principle which Ast has proposed
> and in several respects developed quite extensively is
> that just as the whole is understood from the parts, so
> the parts can be understood only from the whole.
> This principle is of such consequence for
> hermeneutics and so incontestable that one cannot
> even begin to interpret without using it.[32]

Unfortunately, this notion of the hermeneutical circle has created universal concern without universal acceptance.

Criticisms and Clarification

A particularly challenging criticism is made by Richard Palmer, a former student of Gadamer's and a critic of Schleiermacher's idea of the hermeneutical circle. Palmer charges Schleiermacher with a logical contradiction. Palmer begins with a review of Schleiermacher's theory of interpretation.[33] Schleiermacher's starting point explains how it is possible for any or all utterance, whether spoken or written, to be understood. It is impossible without a dialogical relationship, i.e. a communal context, in which any and all utterances have meaning.

Understanding, according to Schleiermacher, is reexperiencing the mental processes of the text's author. It is the opposite of composition because it starts with the finished product and attempts to return to the mental life from which the product arose. Interpretation, therefore, consists of two interacting moments: the grammatical and the psychological. These two poles form the hermeneutical circle. According to Palmer, however, the hermeneutical circle seems logically contradictory.[34] Because understanding cannot fully account for the workings of understanding, a leap into the hermeneutical circle occurs and we are then able to

---

[32] Ibid., p. 75.
[33] Palmer, Richard E. Hermeneutics: Interpretation Theory in Schleiermacher, Dilthey, Heidegger and Gadamer. Evanston, IL: Northwestern University Press, 1969, p.85.
[34] Ibid., p. 87.

understand the whole and the parts together.

This, and other criticisms similar to it, fail to recognize the emphasis Schleiermacher placed on the provisional and imperfect understanding which are present at the start of the study of a text. These imperfections are gradually overcome in the course of working to understand the text. In fact, the parts place limitations on what the whole can mean and the meaning of the whole can only be that which best ties the parts of a work together into the most coherent, plausible structure.[35]

In defense of Schleiermacher, Richard Corliss and others have noted that Schleiermacher's concern is to demonstrate the unity between two acts of interpretation which contemporary hermeneutics split apart. Linguistically-oriented interpreters focus on the relation of an individual work to others of similar genre, while author-oriented interpreters focus on what kind of person the author is who wrote the work. What Schleiermacher endeavors to do is to combine both linguistic-oriented and author-oriented interpretations in the construction and apprehension of communal understanding.

Schleiermacher's 'hermeneutical circle,' therefore, is an excellent example of the interpretive role played by the religious community. Using Schleiermacher's scheme, we can see that meaning gathers momentum as the individual works to 'make sense' of his or her individual experience and perspective. As one moves out, moreover, the 'hermeneutical circle' must expand to become an ascending spiral and not an ellipse.

The idea of an ascending spiral is driven by what provides the best explanation for the parts. This is the unifying ideal. Schleiermacher is not advocating that language is only self-revelatory and meaning an internal working out. Schleiermacher is suggesting that the ultimate purpose of hermeneutics is to provide a unifying, overarching meaning which holds contingent, historical experiences together in a way that makes the most sense.

Schleiermacher's strongest critic, Hans Georg Gadamer, sees interpretation, in part, as the activity of humans in shaping their understanding of

---

[35] Corliss, Richard L. "Schleiermacher's Hermeneutic and Its Critics," <u>Religious Studies,</u> Cambridge, Eng., 1993, vol. 29, pp. 363-379.

a text or a situation. Interpretation, according to Gadamer, reveals the structure of our being as humans. Understanding occurs because the interpretation of any text or situation is fundamentally accomplished by the pre-understanding one brings to the situation. In condemning Schleiermacher, Gadamer emphasizes that, "the circle of understanding is...an ontological structural element in understanding."[36]

Again, this presentation of Schleiermacher's hermeneutics fails to appreciate that Schleiermacher is pursuing a different project. Gadamer attempts to analyze the nature of human reality while Schleiermacher attempts to explicate how human consciousness is formed, communicated, and understood through language.[37] As Schleiermacher repeatedly emphasizes, he wants to determine how human communication is possible at all, not what human communication reveals about the nature of humans. In this respect, Schleiermacher suggests that language is not only a bridge between people, but between people and the realm of ultimate, unifying ideals.

In introducing Schleiermacher's theory of hermeneutics, David Klemm highlights four aspects of Schleiermacher's approach, two of which are relevant for our purposes here. First, Klemm highlights that Schleiermacher always began by asking the dual question: What is the intention of the author and how would the original audience have understood this intention?[38] Thus, texts have a core, objective meaning which reflects the way in which the community understands its embodiment of the ideal. As texts give shape to a particular communal consciousness, so the communal consciousness determines which texts will become authoritative in preserving the community's understanding of its unifying ideals.

Second, hermeneutics is a practical philosophy of ethics which demonstrates how understanding occurs. By identifying the basic ways in which the process of understanding unfolds, one is able to distill the fundamental ways in which humans should interact with themselves and their world. Elsewhere,

---

[36] Gadamer, Hans Georg. <u>Truth and Method.</u> London: Sheed and Ward, 1975, p. 261.

[37] Corliss, R. <u>op. cit.</u>, p. 377.

[38] Klemm, D. <u>op. cit.</u> ,p. 34.

Schleiermacher demonstrates the way in which human action both sustains particular communities and forms bridges between contingent experiences and the unity of their meaning in an overarching ideal.

Klemm suggests this point in his introduction to Schleiermacher's Academy Addresses. Here, Klemm notes that Schleiermacher's emphasis shifts to how thought which is expressed in discourse has a twofold reference to the objective meaning in the context of the entire language and to the specific thought in the entire life of the author. It is this combination of thought and language revealed through discourse which reflects the unifying ideal of the community. This ideal is affirmed and embraced through the formation of a bond of interpretation between the individual and the communal ideal.[39]

Because individuals are historically determined their understanding is also historically determined.[40] One's understanding, moreover, can only emerge in history through the use of specific languages. Languages are not timeless, but reflect the influence of time and culture, tradition and place.[41] Religious understanding, moreover, can only be appropriated through the use of language in a particular time and culture, a specific tradition and place. Religious understanding, therefore, emerges in the context of specific religious communities which shape particular forms of religious consciousness through their specific uses of language.

The Importance of Oral and Written Forms of Language Use

Language is a fundamental element in the creation and development of religious consciousness. A specific religious consciousness is created and perpetuated through particular language uses distilled in religious doctrines. Religious doctrine, in turn, utilizes language in a specific way to shape self-consciousness through the activity of interpretation contextualized within a

---

[39] Ibid., pp. 55-58.
[40] Niebuhr, R.R. "Schleiermacher on Language and Feeling," Theology Today, Vol. 17, p. 150, 1960-61. Princeton Theological Seminary.
[41] Ibid., p. 152.

particular community.[42]

The religious community helps provide the communal context within which an individual can understand and interpret their specific religious experiences. In this context, the way in which language is used fundamentally determines the kind and degree of individual religious consciousness which develops. Individual religious consciousness awakens in accordance with the types of rituals, traditions and language activities which reflect and perpetuate the understanding of reality transmitted by a specific religious community.[43]

The religious consciousness created and sustained by the Christian religious community is the feeling of absolute dependence on God as manifested in the life of Jesus. This feeling is awakened within the religious community through language use and corporate activities communicated and stimulated by individual speech acts and communal ritual activities. A primary vehicle for communicating and stimulating the feeling of absolute dependence, moreover, is preaching.

Schleiermacher defines the role of preaching in a specific, illuminating way. Preaching is responsible for awakening one's need for redemption and helping the one subsequently awakened to find satisfaction for this need in the redemption accomplished by identifying with the God-consciousness of Jesus of Nazareth.[44] Preaching is a bond-building activity. Because faith does not spring from proof but from preaching, and preaching only occurs in the context of the church, the bonds of faith cannot develop unless one is a participant in a community of faith.[45]

The development of faith is linked immediately with participation in the religious community. Faith is a spontaneous response to the spontaneous stimulus of preaching. Without preaching, human consciousness would never develop to the point where it could respond, with understanding, to the meaning of Jesus as

---

[42] Schleiermacher, F. The Christian Faith. p. 118, #28.

[43] Ibid., p. 160.

[44] Ibid., p. 69, #14.1.

[45] Ibid., p. 70, #14.3. Pannenberg makes a similar point in his book, The Church, when he writes, "...there is no such thing as a church-less Christian." Pannenberg, Wolfhart. The Church. Translated by Keith Crim. Philadelphia: Westminster Press, 1983.

the Redeemer.   Without preaching, Christianity would not be able to transmit its understanding of the Redeemer nor interpret this meaning to subsequent generations.   Through preaching, moreover, one's religious self-consciousness, shaped by the self-consciousness of the Redeemer, can spiral up to higher levels of communal religious consciousness.   Thus, Schleiermacher's belief that the agnosticism of the 'cultured despisers' of Christianity arises more from their isolation from regular religious stimulation through preaching than from anything else.   They are not in a place where the drive or need for contact with a unifying ideal is evident.

Schleiermacher believes, moreover, that the earliest Christian writings not only establish the standard for all future understandings of Christian faith, but also reflect the religious consciousness which was shaped by the preaching of Jesus and the first disciples.   For example, Schleiermacher demonstrates that the earliest samples of Christian preaching are those preserved in the New Testament, attributed to Jesus Christ, and reflective of the religious self-consciousness of Jesus.[46]   Christ's preaching established early Christian doctrine.   Together, Jesus' preaching and the early doctrinal formation based on his preaching helped establish the way in which subsequent generations in the Christian church would understand the role of preaching in the formation of religious consciousness.

Preaching, as developed by Schleiermacher, is meant to promote the spontaneous and active development of the religious consciousness.[47]   When subsequent generations preach, they stimulate the cultivation and development of religious consciousness by providing bridges between the contingency of their experience and the ultimate ideal as preserved in the church.   Schleiermacher writes,

> ...We are indeed aware that the preaching of Christ which continually sounds forth from the Church is a living and not unfruitful influence: we see the operations of preparatory grace thus beginning in individuals. We see these individuals going on to become members of the Church whose advancing

---

[46] Ibid., p. 81.
[47] Ibid., p. 87.

sanctification   leaves   no   doubt   as   to   their
justification.[48]

As a result, contemporary preaching, as a reflection of Christ's preaching, perpetuates the spontaneous influence of Christ on the participants of the religious community.

Preaching reflects the individual faith of the proclaimer. Faith awakens and develops through preaching and preaching   always originates in the God-consciousness of Jesus Christ. Thus, Christ's example in preaching is to present the consciousness of His absolute awareness of God in order to establish that every subsequent form of preaching must communicate and perpetuate this same religious awareness in the members of the religious community.[49]

The question this raises, however, is why preaching has an unequal effect on the religious consciousness of members in the same religious community. Schleiermacher believes the reason is a natural one. He writes,

> ...different levels of receptivity to the Christian message, by which some are immediately affected and others not, can only be rooted in one's earlier manner of life, and thus are explicable in natural terms.[50]

In other words, the disposition of one's heart through prior preparation will determine the receptivity to the God-consciousness of Jesus communicated through preaching. One must feel the need to understand if one will also feel the need for interpretation. Schleiermacher concludes by explaining that the plight of the human is not one of double predestination, whereby some are ordained for heaven and some for hell. Rather, the plight of humans is to recognize that the blessedness of grace is bestowed to all but realized in varying degrees because of the level to which one has become open to the interpretation of life's realities

---

[48] Ibid., p. 547.
[49] Ibid., p. 564.
[50] Ibid.,#117.

through the unifying ideal which confers divine grace.[51]

---

[51] Moore, Walter L., "Schleiermacher as a Calvinist," <u>Scottish Journal of Theology,</u> Cambridge, Eng: Cambridge University Press, vol. 24, 1971, p. 175.

Chapter Three

The Nature of Interpretation in Royce

Schleiermacher has demonstrated that the societal pressure for ongoing interpretation is acute. Every age must make sense of its own set of unique problems. In order to retain the relevance of its religious symbols a religious community must engage in ongoing interpretation. But how does one determine what should be retained and extended and what should be jettisoned and ignored? Royce, in extending Schleiermacher's treatment of hermeneutics, articulates his theory of interpretation in an effort to show the way in which the religious community can provide both an element of change and an element of permanence that can provide guidance for this process of change.

The starting point in our consideration of the nature of interpretation in Royce is found in his emphasis on developing a theology which extends a tradition. Through this emphasis, Royce advocates an extension through interpretation of a previously articulated religious tradition.[52] Thus, Royce's argument is for an extended interpretation of Christianity in which one can move beyond a theology *bound* by a tradition to a theology *deeply informed* by a tradition but still able to be extended.[53]

Coherence and Contingency in Royce's Theory of Interpretation

Central to Royce's theory of interpretation are the dual ideas of coherence and contingency. Coherence is the capacity the religious community displays to provide a stable, coherent framework within which one understands and interprets the contingent religious experiences of its personal life. This coherent framework is held together by a network of symbolic relations which reflect a common, universal understanding mediated by the particular community.

---

[52] Cady, Linnell E. "A Model for a Public Theology," Harvard Theological Review, 80:193-212, April, 1987, p. 202.
[53] Ibid., p. 206.

Contingency, by contrast, is the variable, transient element. Contingency reflects the individual, on his or her own, trying to make sense of the multiplicity of individual experiences. There is no unifying thread. But contingency is important because it is here that one's first awakening to the need to find an ultimate explanation arises. If left without a unifying insight, however, one's contingent experiences remain a part of the thick fog of a pluralistic universe.

Royce provides ample illustrations of the way in which the coherent framework of the religious community provides the horizons within which our contingent religious experiences can make sense. For example, perception is an individual sense datum which reflects change and is able to be apprehended immediately. Conception, by contrast, is universal construct of general quality or type which reflects a coherent constancy in one's understanding. Left on one's own, only the Kantian dilemma of empty concepts and blind percepts remains. Interpretation, therefore, between isolated percepts and universal, but empty concepts is necessary if understanding is to occur.[54]

Thus, interpretation is able to draw a synthesis between one's particular perceptions and one's universal conceptions. For example, when I am driving I have *perceptions* of green, yellow and red lights. From my training as a driver I have *concepts* of proceeding, slowing down and stopping. Together, through my community of interpretation, I come to understand that green means to proceed, yellow means to slow down and red means to stop. Without this interpretation, however, it is impossible to demonstrate the relationship between my perception of colored lights and my conception of movement and rest.[55] Likewise, it is impossible for an individual who is isolated from a community of interpretation to find meaning for his or her particular perceptions of religious experience without the broader conceptions provided by the religious community.

In proposing the ideas of coherence and contingency as the dual realities in the activity of interpretation, one is able to see how Royce ties the present with the past in the context of community.[56] It is the interpretive activity of the

---

[54] Royce, J. The Problems of Christianity, vol. II, pp. 127-128.
[55] Ibid., p. 118.
[56] Ibid., p. 47.

community which binds the contingent variety of one's personal religious experiences with the coherent meaning contextualized within this community. Through the coherence one gains by identifying with a particular community, it is possible to obtain a unifying ideal which can draw all individual experiences into a coherent whole through interpretation.[57] In essence, Royce is arguing that there is a unity to the life of an individual self because there is a unity to the life of the community of interpretation of which the self is a part. Being able to provide this unity of life is the central goal and purpose of interpretation.

To extend this idea further, Royce suggests that there is both a momentary self and an ideal self. The momentary self is depicted as fleeting and tied to the daily variety of specific activities. The ideal self, by contrast, provides continuity over time. It is the ideal self, not the momentary self, which is formed from the interpretive activity of the religious community.

To illustrate this same sense of coherence and contingency, Royce draws an example from the way in which the scientific community evaluates and accepts new discoveries. An individual scientist, as contingent, makes a discovery. This individual discovery is significant, but unless it can be verified and repeated by other scientists it will remain an individual discovery without communal acceptance. If one is able to move from individual discovery to communal acceptance through the interpretive process, then the interpretive framework provided by the scientific community can verify and accept the contingent individual discovery into its corporate consciousness.[58]

But what forms the foundation of these mediating links? Essentially, it is the result not only of one definite event which all members of the community relate to as a community, but also the manner in which each individual member subsequently interprets his or her relationship to the community as a whole. Royce states that a very definite event must be viewed by each member of the community as a part of his or her personal salvation.[59] Without a single, defining event the community would lose its basis of coherence.

---

[57] Ibid., p. 46.
[58] Ibid., pp. 231-233.
[59] Ibid., p. 71.

But there is more than merely the historical validity of this one event. The event must be interpreted to have meaning and this interpretation reflects the dynamic of interpretation embedded in the corporate consciousness of the religious community. The act of interpretation is the act of forming a coherent and plausible picture from a variety of contingent experiences which otherwise remain ambiguous. The Apostle Paul, for example, interpreted religious traditions in such a way that he was able to articulate both the goal of each individual person and the anticipated outcome of the entire race. [60] His role as an interpreter was to stand in the gap and form a bridge of understanding over which one might pass from confusion to meaning.

These processes of interpretation, moreover, are possible because of the establishment of the religious community. [61] The continuity of a community depends on the way in which each of its individual members interprets his or her individual life. [62] Interpretation, as a mental process, permits one to utilize the artifacts of language and culture to construct meaningful interpretations of their religious experience. [63] If isolated from the community of discourse, however, these experiences remain as random artifacts devoid of meaning.

In articulating his understanding of interpretation, moreover, Royce borrows from Kant, but with an important change. Kant had argued that a triadic distinction exists between sense, understanding and reason. Sense, for Kant, is similar to Royce's definition of percepts. Understanding, for Kant, is similar to Royce's definition of concepts. But reason, as Kant defines it, must be expanded in order to fit within Royce's description of interpretation. [64]

The necessary expansion within Kant's system is the role imagination plays as an expression of autonomous reason. Through this expansion of reason, a framework is constructed within the transcendental ego by which human understanding can occur. Kant defined imagination as that which extracts from

---

[60] Ibid., p. 77.
[61] Ibid., p. 109.
[62] Ibid., p. 111.
[63] Ibid., p. 117.
[64] Ibid., p. 120.

lived experience the framework within which these experiences can occur.[65]

Imagination is the power within the human which generates possible explanations for how and why we experience life the way we do. It creates understanding. It clarifies meaning. It permits the noumenal and phenomenal selves to connect with one another. Without imagination, we would never be able to know,[66] understand or even conceptualize our experience of the world.[67] Imagination, as an activity of reason, operates to synthesize the specific experiences of an individual's life into a unified, meaningful whole.[68] But this all occurs within the domain of autonomous reason.

Thus, Royce enlarges Kant's understanding of reason activated by imagination to show how reason, in the context of the religious community, is a more sufficient explanation for how interpretation operates to integrate opposing forces into a meaningful whole. In discussing Kant's position, Royce is careful to show that the activity Kant identifies with the transcendental unity of apperception is similar to the activity Royce identifies with the processes of interpretation within community.[69] The important difference between Kant and Royce, however, is that for Kant this activity transpires within the individual mind whereas for Royce it happens in and through the interpretive community. As a result, Royce defines the activity of interpretation as the quest to obtain meaning and understanding through the interpretive role of the religious community.

Interpretation is communal and triadic.[70] There is an interpreter, that which is interpreted and an interpretee, the one to whom the interpreter directs his or her interpretation. This triadic structure allows meaning-giving and understanding-transmitting interpretation to occur because of its contextualization within community.[71]

Because the process of interpretation is inherently social, a bridge is

---

[65] Kant, Immanuel. The Critique of Pure Reason. Translated by Norman Kemp Smith. New York: St. Martin's Press, 1965.
[66] Ibid., p. 112.
[67] Ibid., p. 127.
[68] Ibid., pp. 142-43.
[69] Royce, Problem of Christianity, vl. II, p. 125.
[70] Ibid., p. 140.
[71] Ibid., p. 148.

formed between our individual percepts and our universal concepts by the religious community.[72] Interpretation, therefore, is an essentially endless process unless disrupted by personal demise or the complete annihilation of the community in which this history of interpretation is embedded.[73] That is to say, every historic community, religious, or otherwise, has transforming potential within it. If understood properly, every community has the power to stand not only for itself, but also as a conduit on the way to the 'Beloved Community.'

Royce offers an analogy to illustrate this understanding. In this analogy, Royce identifies a traveler who comes to the border of a new country and must exchange his gold coins and paper currency for the currency of the new country he desires to enter. Through this illustration, Royce identifies the way in which an interpretation becomes a new reality extended beyond the objects which gave rise to the initial interpretation.

In this story, the traveler faces a unique challenge. On the one hand, the easiest way for the traveler to exchange his money would be a one-to-one correspondence with the country he is entering. For example, if he was traveling from the United States to England, he would exchange one U.S. dollar for one British pound. The standard currency of one country would be exchanged straight across for the standard currency of the other country. But this is not possible.

Equally problematic for the traveler would be if he was forced to exchange one pound (in weight) of his coins and currency for one British pound (in currency). In this second scenario, the value, or the meaning, of the U.S. currency is completely lost in its exchange for British currency. Both depictions fail to solve the traveler's dilemma in exchanging the value of his currency for equal value in the currency of the new country.

To solve his dilemma, the traveler must interpret between the value of his present currency and the equal value of the currency of the country he is entering. Through interpretation he is able to determine that one U.S. dollar is equivalent to 1.4 British pounds. In order to accomplish this interpretation the traveler must

---

[72] Ibid., p. 49.
[73] Ibid., p. 150. A classic example of the threat of communal annihilation is the Holocaust. No other event in recent history distills the efforts of one group, the Nazis, to annihilate the meaning of interpretation of another group, the Jews.

rely on the community of interpretation, in this case, the International Monetary Exchange Board, to establish the exchange value between the two currencies.

This analogy lies at the very heart of Royce's interpretation of Christianity. It extends the theory of interpretation of Schleiermacher to show the way in which acts of interpretation extend the context of community. If there is any danger with Royce's theory it is the fear that in moving into a new mind set and exchanging the currency into the new mind set one may exchange old currency for new currency which inevitably goes bankrupt. Nevertheless, this analogy reflects Royce's operating premise that the responsibility of interpretation is to be deeply informed by a tradition while extending the tradition. That is, the traveler preserves the value of his former currency by exchanging it for equivalent value in the new currency. To interpret the doctrines of Christianity is to take the essence and meaning of these doctrines and form a bridge of understanding through interpretation, which carries one into the new country. The value remains the same, but the currency which carries the value has changed.

The traveler, as Royce's archetype of Christianity, has come to the border of a new country, the modern mentality, and must exchange his old currency for currency which will be accepted in the new country. The currency carries the value reflective of the beliefs and doctrines central to Christianity. Thus, the value, or meanings, attached to the old currency will not change, but the content, or currency, in which these meanings are carried must change. Finally, the adequacy of the new currency to carry the same meaning will endure only until the traveler must leave the present country in order to travel to a new country or mind set. As a result, when Royce turns to the doctrines of Christianity in order to cull their essential meanings, he does so with the intent of translating these historic meanings into contemporary currency for a new mind set.[74]

It is the community which provides the mediating context within which an individual, who has awakened to his or her need for a new interpretation, can find the tools necessary to make a new interpretation which preserves the essential value. Through interpretation, the individual achieves a larger unity of

---

[74] Ibid., p. 130 ff.

consciousness through the bridge-building context of the particular community.[75] Since the essence of interpretation is mediation, it is the mediating activity of interpretation within the mediating context of community that provides understanding. As an example of the mediating and community forming activity of interpretation, Royce offers the example of the interpreter who, in his effort to explain an ancient text, is able to unite two minds in understanding through his act of interpretation.

In offering this illustration, Royce provides a helpful example of how the formation of doctrines can preserve historically derived meanings in a coherent form for future manifestations within a community. As Royce notes, when one interprets a text, there is a text, the one who interprets the text and the one to whom the text is interpreted. In order for adequate understanding to occur the interpreter must understand not only the text and the context in which it was constructed, but also the mind set and context of the one to whom the text is being interpreted.

This is possible because the community of interpretation provides the context within which the meaning of both the ancient text and the modern translation can be understood. In this way, doctrines are formed which distill new understandings. The desire, or will, to provide this interpretation is critical to community formation. The will-to-interpret forms a community between the interpreter, the interpretee and the item interpreted by interpreter to interpretee.[76] Thus, the community of interpretation, which reflects the social nature of interpretation, is the process by which three selves are interpreted to one another and derive a new understanding through the interpretive process of the community.[77]

Royce identifies the will-to-interpret with his position of absolute volunteerism. Absolute volunteerism understands that ultimately there is only one right attitude of the will to the universe. It suggests that there is only one

---

[75]Oppenheimer, Frank. "A Roycean Road to Community." International Philosophical Quarterly. 10, pp. 341-377, Sept., 1970, p. 342.

[76] Royce, J. The Problem of Christianity, vol. II., p. 208.

[77] Ibid., p. 211.

ultimate, unifying ideal. This is the pearl of great price for which everyone who awakens to his or her religious need must seek. When initiated, the will-to-interpret leads to the formation of a community of interpretation based on the way in which the spirit of loyalty has become embodied in historic form in the community. This attitude of the will is the one which Paul identified with charity and gave rise to the first Christian communities clustered around the ultimate ideal of loyalty to a cause.[78]

As the community of interpretation is formed it also develops. As a community, it spirals up through various stages of religious consciousness seeking to find the ultimate, unifying ideal for its life. As it moves from primitive religious consciousness through creedal development to integration of faith and practice and finally, the religion of loyalty expressed as the Beloved Community, it ascends towards its unifying ideal.[79] This ideal provides a sustainable and plausible explanation for the contingent experiences of an individual's life.

As an individual, the discovery of the 'Beloved Community' follows this four-fold process. First, one captures the ideal of interpretation as the dynamic spiritual force emanating throughout the universe. Second, the community of interpretation is formed by all who have recognized this dynamic and seek to integrate others, as they themselves have been integrated, into the universal community of interpretation. Third, the community of interpretation is unified by the common hope of a universal community of common interpretation in which the social and interpretive nature of reality can be celebrated and embraced. And finally, as love for the ideal of a universal community is awakened, pursuit of this ideal is commenced.[80] It is through the process of interpretation that the purest form of individual love for interpretive communities can develop.[81]

---

[78] Ibid., p. 325.
[79] Royce, Josiah. William James and Other Essays on the Philosophy of Life. New York: Macmillan Company, 1911, pp. 118-121.
[80] Royce, J. The Problem of Christianity, p. 220.
[81] Royce, Josiah. The Problem of Christianity. p. 218.

The Role of Signs in the Process of Interpretation

By the end of his career, Royce had developed an elaborate sign system which explained his view of the role of the community of interpretation. Royce borrowed heavily from C. S. Peirce in establishing the inherently triadic nature of interpretation. There were three selves or signs of selves in every act of interpretation. Every act of interpretation includes a self or sign interpreted, the interpreter, and the one who receives the interpretation.[82] Since the central knowing activity is interpretation and since interpretation is always an endless social activity, the central knowing activity is always an endless social activity.

What Royce tries to illustrate is the way in which the interpretive process creates the relations we enjoy within community. Signs are a form of interpretive bridges. They act as mediating realities between our individual experiences and the meaning these experiences have in our broader social context.[83]

Our religious experiences occur in the realm of signs. As such, these signs allow us to make sense of our experiences by placing them within a broader framework of a community in which they can be interpreted. Every new interpretation forms a new sign thereby launching the endless activity of interpretation.

John E. Smith offers the following analysis of Royce's theory of the endless nature of interpretation. If x=any sign to be interpreted, y=any interpreter, and z=any interpretee, then y's interpretation of x to z forms a new interpretation, I. I is the new sign reflecting the triadic relation of x, y, and z. But once I is formed then it becomes a new sign requiring interpretation by yI to zI. And thus, the interpretive process goes on endlessly until reaching its final consummation in the 'Beloved Community.'[84]

The significance of Smith's explanation is the way in which he shows the bond-forming nature of interpretation. Interpretation allows for unities to form between past understandings, present meanings and future needs.

---

[82] Oppenheimer, Frank. op. cit., p.345.
[83] Royce, J. The Problem of Christianity, vol. II, p. 283.
[84] Smith, John E. Royce's Social Infinite. New York: Liberal Arts Press, 1950, p. 88.

The One Event

Because Royce believes the process of interpreting one event forms the spiritual dynamic of every religious community, he identifies the origination of this dynamic with Paul's interpretation of the life and ministry of Jesus Christ. This interpretation is more significant than the particular history of Jesus Christ because it is this interpretation which takes Jesus Christ out of his country of first-century Rabbinic Palestine and preserves the meaning of his message by exchanging the currency of Judaism into the universal currency of the Early Church. Through Paul's interpretation of the meaning and purpose of the crucifixion and resurrection of Jesus, the Early Church was formed into the Body of Christ and commenced a new mind set in the history of religions.[85] This new mind set was fashioned not on the particular preference of a monotheistic God, but on the universal expression of loyalty to a new understanding.

Royce is careful to note that the interpreted event must take on historical, concrete form.[86] In other words, every historical, contingent reality is a sign which must be interpreted. But, for Royce, this historical, concrete sign is not the person of Jesus, but the Christ-spirit formed by the interpretation of the Pauline church. This historical, concrete sign, moreover, is a sign found in every manifestation of the religion of loyalty. For the Christian and the Christian community, the spirit of Christ is the sustaining spiritual reality experienced when the signs of religious experience are interpreted within the religious community.[87] Salvation, therefore, is mediated not by Jesus, but by the Christ-spirit that draws all who seek into unity through interpretation.

Royce continues by noting that it is the historical fact of the community clustered around its interpretation of Christ that draws the loyal towards realization of a universal community of loyalty in which all are saved.[88] In an effort to exchange the currency of Orthodox doctrines concerning Jesus for currency adequate to the modern mind set, Royce advocates an interpretation of

---

[85] Ibid., p. 80.
[86] Ibid., p. 426.
[87] Ibid., p. 215.
[88] ibid., p. 425.

the Christ-event, as a sign, which breeds devotion to the spirit of loyalty grounded in the universal and 'Beloved Community.'[89]

The consequence of this interpretation, moreover, is its identification of salvation with the practical devotion of an individual to a cause. The practical devotion of an individual to a cause creates contact with the sign-signifying power of the community. By coming into contact with the community, the Christ-spirit can activate to interpret between individual experiences and collective ideals. This is the universal core value of all religions. Religions differ according to kind and degree because of the accidents of race and nation, and the constructive contributions mediated by styles of worship, doctrinal teaching, and religious training.[90] But when these contingent signs are peeled away, the kernel of religion is found not in the person of Jesus, nor in the purported sayings of Jesus, nor in any other individual; these are all signs pointing to a greater reality. No, it is not in the signs, but in their interpretation that one enters the community of the faithful in which all who are loyal to their cause will be saved.[91]

Thus, the coherent center of Christian faith is the sign-interpreting spirit of the Beloved Community. This is where grace works to atone past deeds through the saving power of the loyal spirit.[92] If one recognizes the validity of this interpretation as the universal purpose of all human religion then one will emerge beyond the outmoded currency of one's former understandings. In exchange for their old currency, a new currency is given which mediates meaning to all who are loyal.

There is no final form of Christianity or of any other religion. Progress towards realization of one universal religion remains a distant ideal. One can only hope for a time when religion will find a form in which all of its historically contingent signs can form a common basis for all subsequent interpretation.[93] For now, Christianity has provided us with the best single set of signs which, through interpretation, exchange contextual, parochial understandings without ultimate

---

[89] Ibid., p. 428.
[90] Ibid., pp. 428-429.
[91] Ibid., p. 428.
[92] Ibid., p. 429.
[93] Ibid., p. 432.

meaning into universal currency held by all who are loyal.

Royce concludes his articulation of the core event of Christianity by emphasizing that the particularity of Jesus, as a sign, is inseparable from the essential spirit present in the true church.[94] It is the common social experience of the community which can mediate the spirit of Christ through interpretation. This mediation, moreover, is a sign which connects the individual with the community in order that the collective consciousness of the community can provide a unifying ideal for all who are loyal.

To amplify this point, Royce notes that Paul's focus in I Corinthians 15 is to interpret the resurrection of Christ as foreshadowing the common resurrection of all.[95] What Paul is teaching, according to Royce, is that the sign of the resurrection of Christ is significant only as a symbol of the common resurrection of all who are faithful.[96] According to Royce's interpretation of Paul, the individual is saved only through the interpretation of this sign which releases the universal spirit and grafts the individual into the community and its Lord.[97]

The Founder of Christianity

Because the founder of Christianity is more than Jesus or Paul, Royce seeks to demonstrate the metaphysical foundation of reality which Christianity has captured. Even if Christianity did not exist, the ideas expressed by Christianity would have found some other sign form in which these realities could be expressed.[98] Historically, the Christian church was the first group to discover these metaphysical truths. Although Jesus is often viewed as the founder of Christianity, this is an erroneous judgment since Jesus' teachings do not define these ideas adequately or clearly. Rather, Jesus' teachings form the signs which were subsequently interpreted by Paul in the context of the Early Church. Indeed, it is Paul's interpretation of the signs provided by Christ's life and teachings

---

[94] Ibid., p. 359.
[95] Ibid., p. 73.
[96] Ibid., p. 76.
[97] Ibid., p. 78.
[98] Royce, Josiah. The Problem of Christianity, vol. I, p. XX.

which formed the Early Church[99]   Unfortunately, however, liberal and orthodox alike have missed the meaning of the sign-interpreting activity of Paul and the Early Church.

The liberal has made the mistake of believing that Jesus is a pound (in weight) of U.S. currency which must be exchanged for one pound (in currency) of British currency. In other words, what meaning and value the currency once held no longer has any correspondence with the meaning and value of the new currency. The liberal has missed the interpretive meaning of the sign.

The orthodox has made an equally disastrous mistake by believing that Jesus is one dollar of U.S. currency which can be exchanged straight across for one British pound. In other words, the meaning and value the currency held in one country, or mind set, corresponds directly to the meaning and value of the currency of the new country, or mind set. Thus, no interpretation can occur and if no interpretation occurs, no meaning is given.

What must be recognized it that both interpretations reflect an entirely misplaced focus. The orthodox has tried to transmit a timeless understanding of Jesus' person and work without accounting for either the dynamics within a new context or the challenges to old interpretations confronted by a new religious community. The images and understandings we have of Jesus are multifarious. Even the Early Church had a multitude of interpretations of Jesus.[100]   The goal is not to ignore this multiplicity, but to determine what overarching ideal can draw this contingency into coherent unity.

The liberal is equally misguided because he or she believes if one could only peel away the multitude of images and interpretations one could ascertain the 'real, historical' Jesus, the provincial carpenter of Nazareth, or whatever. One would then be able to identify and express the true meaning of Christianity. But the true essence of Christianity is its interpretation of signs which give rise to the religion of loyalty. These signs are found in individuals, interpreted across mind

---

[99] Ibid., p. XXI.
[100] See, Brown, Raymond and John P. Meyer. Antioch and Rome:New Testament Cradles for Catholic Christianity (New York: Paulist Press, 1983), and Jaroslav Pelikan, Jesus Through the Centuries (New York: Harper and Row, Publishers, 1985). These two books are indicative of the vast array of literature in both Biblical Studies and Historical Theology which highlight this point.

sets and safeguarded by the universal Beloved Community as symbolized in the Early Church.[101]

Thus, the veracity of Christianity's interpretation is grounded in its ability to retain its inherent value while being exchanged for the currency of a new mind set. In other words, neither Jesus nor Paul founded Christianity, but the Christian community, as the context of sign interpretation, released the Christ-spirit through which Paul could interpret the life and ministry of Jesus as loyalty to a supreme cause, the Beloved Community.[102]

The signs which distill the essence of Jesus must be interpreted in each new mind set. The true essence of Christianity is, therefore, its realization of the need for endless interpretation of contingent signs in order to build bridges and develop bonds which connect the autonomous individual with the true nature of reality anchored to the universal Beloved Community.[103] This is the essence of Pauline Christianity which captured the meaning of the person of Christ as a sign to be interpreted across the time process of history.[104]

According to Royce, Christ was for Paul the interpretation of the signs provided by Jesus' teaching which exists as the indwelling spirit of the religious community.[105] Through Paul's interpretation of the signs of Christ, the church was able to embrace Christ's death and resurrection as the symbol for the way in which the community could communicate divine grace.[106] This divine grace could only be experienced and realized through the loyalty to the Beloved Community mediated by the signs embodied in the teachings of Jesus.[107]

Paul's interpretation translates contingent signs into overarching ideals which form communities. These communities, moreover, become repositories for future interpretations and manifest the spirit of loyalty in which the communities

---

[101] Problem, vol. II, xxv.
[102] Problem, vol. II, p. 30.
[103] Problem, vol. I, p. xxv.
[104] Royce, J. The Problem of Christianity, vol. II, p. 362.
[105] Ibid., p. 369.
[106] Royce, J. PC, vol. I, p. 187.
[107] Ibid., p. 199. In the Preface to The Problem of Christianity, Royce expresses his deep debt to Ernst Troeltsch and The Social Teaching of the Christian Churches. Here, Troeltsch's influence is apparent and striking.

of loyalty can become visible and tangible, and, therefore, part of the sign process.[108] As such, these interpretations within community recreate signs of the risen Lord which allow new individuals to come in contact with the Christ-spirit and be saved.

The Christian church, as the visible embodiment of the spirit of loyalty, has encountered two specific challenges to its understanding of the religious life subsequent to Paul. First, the Christian church has had to explain how the visible manifestation of the invisible ideal could fall so far short of its stated vision. Second, the church has had to provide an adequate understanding of the relation between its ideal of a spirit of loyalty and the concrete, historical reality of the person and teaching of Jesus.[109]

In response to both of these challenges, Christianity has, according to Royce, demonstrated that one individual has solved that mystery for all time.[110] But this individual is not Jesus, but the risen Christ as the sign interpreted by Paul in giving rise to the earliest Christian communities.[111] The teachings of Jesus are simply the words of the Christian community read back into his person to communicate its own ideals. When Jesus states, in John 14, "...Peace I leave with you, my peace I give unto you;..." these words reflect the ideal voice of the saving community and not the actual voice of an individual savior.[112] These words, moreover, are temporal signs which embody the living spirit of the universal ideal.

In the final analysis, Royce notes that it must be true that Jesus, during his natural life, taught a doctrine which made the first Christian community possible.[113] But it is not necessary to believe this to be true. We need only recognize the role of Jesus by seeing him as the temporal sign who gave impetus

---

[108] Ibid., p. 201.

[109] Ibid., pp. 201-202.

[110] Ibid., p. 209.

[111] David Strauss argued strenuously against Schleiermacher in advocating a similar point. Strauss suggested that it is impossible to get back to any reliable history of Jesus and one is left only with the Christ of faith. See Strauss, David F. The Jesus of History and the Christ of Faith: a commentary on Schleiermacher's 'Life of Jesus.' Translated, edited, and with an introduction by Leander Keck. Philadelphia: Fortress Press, 1977.

[112] Problem, vol. I, p. 211.

[113] Ibid., p. 16.

to the emergence of the first Christian community by Paul's interpretation of this sign. It was the community, created by the interpretive activity of Paul, which created the structure within which the unclear and ambiguous implications of Jesus' teachings could unify around the universal ideal of loyalty. Thus, Royce concludes, the founder of Christianity was neither Jesus nor Paul, but the early communities which provided the context in which the meaning of the life and teachings of Jesus, as temporal signs, could be interpreted for all future communities.

Since the community is both the context for interpreting signs and a complex sign itself, a consideration of the nature of communities will follow.

Section II: The Nature of the Community in Schleiermacher and Royce

Chapter Four

The Nature of the Religious Community in Schleiermacher

In Robert Bellah's Habits of the Heart, Bellah recites Alexis de Tocqueville's optimism regarding the American democratic ideal. Of specific interest to Bellah is the way in which de Tocqueville rightly identifies the twin ideals within American life, individualism and equality, but wrongly identifies which one would win out. De Tocqueville believed the compensating forces within American life would allow equality to keep individualism in check and that a certain tempered individualism would emerge from the dynamic interplay of these two guiding ideals. As Bellah notes, just the opposite has occurred.[114]

The Enlightenment ideal of radical individualism has been the guiding ideal of American thought and culture for at least two centuries. The constituting self, as the primary locus of meaning and value, comes before any other social or cultural connections. But this ideal has failed to sustain our civilization.

What Schleiermacher and Royce both recognize, in accord with Bellah's recent observations, is the reality that the Enlightenment ideal of the self is misguided. The idea that individuals are unencumbered by any social ties is erroneous. They contend, further, that we are, fundamentally and always, social creatures and that we cannot live without the shared understandings of our communal identity.

In Schleiermacher's treatment of the nature of the religious community, he works with an understanding of the self in community, which fundamentally rejects Enlightenment individualism.

Schleiermacher's earliest published treatise, On Religion, gained an instant following because of its consideration of the nature of religious experience

---

[114] Bellah, Robert. Habits of the Heart. San Francisco: Harper and Row, Inc., 1986, pp. 3-28.

and the way in which he envisioned the development of religious consciousness. But it was not without its critics. Of particular interest is the treatment he gave the role of the religious community in the interpretation of religious experience. The main source of criticism came from the cultured despisers of Christianity and reflected an overwhelming bias against organized forms of religion. As a result, Schleiermacher saw the way in which one could overlook the vital and central role the religious community plays in the understanding of one's faith.

The Nature and Function of the Religious Community in the Speeches

The religious community, according to Schleiermacher, provoked contempt among his contemporaries.[115] The opposition from Christianity's cultured despisers came, not because of a lack of interest in religion per se, but from an utter contempt for the organized form of religions which many saw as corrupt and unnecessary. Of particular concern was the way in which organized religion stifled personal freedom in its perpetuation of dead customs and its moral bankruptcy as evident from its role as the custodian in some of the worst atrocities in world history.[116]

These responses to organized religion, however, blinded the critics to the fundamental social nature of religion. Religion is, by necessity, social. Humans are social animals and religion is an expression of our fundamental nature as humans. The social context interprets and legitimates religious experience by providing a framework within which individual religious consciousness can awaken and develop and provide the necessary conceptual apparatus for understanding one's own religious experience.[117]

Beginning with Speech Three, Schleiermacher outlines the way in which individual religious experience expands into its communal forms. Schleiermacher works from the inside out. There is a contrast between inner and outer aspects of

---

[115] Schleiermacher, F. On Religion: Speeches to the Cultured Among Its Despisers. Translated from the 1799 edition by Richard Coulter. New York: Cambridge University Press, 1988, p. 162.

[116] Ibid., p. 163.

[117] Ibid.

personal formation. Outer forms are those forms which restrict the development of a religious spirit and, thus, impede a human from developing his or her religious sense fully. By their nature, outer forms, such as the use of language, the role of creeds, and the restraints of communal traditions, inhibit the free movement of the intuition in grasping the infinite.

By contrast, the inner form is the context for the intuition of the infinite which is the essence of religious experience. This intuition lays the foundation for the formation of the self and continual attention to this intuition drives one towards the completion of one's nature. Schleiermacher believes that the human is born with an innate capacity for religion. Within the essence of religion exist two poles which operate in tension with each other: the particular and the universal. Proper formation of the self occurs when a free exchange between these two poles is uninhibited by outer constraints. Interruption of this exchange constitutes a disruption in the formation of the self.

Schleiermacher further believes that an excessive preoccupation with prudent and pragmatic action prevents the individual from finding the universal ideal which can integrate all aspects of personal experience. Those preoccupied with prudent and pragmatic action (and Schleiermacher believes the majority of us are) seek to achieve or finish something only as a project in itself. It is not a sign of something greater which can elevate one. By contrast, those imbued with the religious spirit are engaged in an endless quest for the infinite. This quest involves the whole spirit and, through discipline, reflection, and consistent attention to this quest, one discovers the unifying ideal within which all contingent realities make sense.

Schleiermacher also believes that the shackling of the ego is the only activity which can focus the energies of an individual in his or her movement towards the infinite. The less self-centered one is, the more capable of apprehending the universe one becomes. As one moves closer and closer to a complete intuition of the infinite, an awareness of one's own finitude and eventual death is offset by a feeling of contact with the infinite. Thus, even death becomes not a barrier, but a passageway. It is a sign of a greater reality to be realized through interpretation.

Schleiermacher concludes Speech Three by noting the role art can play as an opening to religious intuition. He admits he has never experienced art in this way and, thus, cannot comment fully on its role in providing a bridge for the individual self to ascend to the realm of universal meaning. Still, he recognizes its proper place as an opening to the infinite and this observation reflects the way in which Schleiermacher contextualized religious experience as an aspect of aesthetic thought.[118]

To illustrate the way in which reflection upon art objects can mediate ultimate ideals, consider this example. You are standing in front of Renoir's, "A Girl with a Watering Can," at the National Gallery in Washington, D.C. You have just spent an hour with your senator wrangling over an issue of vital significance to your region. Initially, you are mad and still upset by his casual indifference to your concern. But as you observe the painting, your mood begins to shift. You are struck by Renoir's use of light and color. You reflect on your lectures from Aesthetics on Impressionism and are moved by his embodiment of these ideas on canvas.

As you reflect, you find yourself caught up in a spirit of ecstasy. You begin to sing softly to yourself. The thought of your senator's casual indifference no longer sickens you. In fact, you begin to see the man, not as a politician, but as a living, breathing human being, full of competing interests, and worthy of your love and respect.

As your ecstasy subsides and your sense of euphoria weakens you notice the lady standing next to you is crying softly. A slow stream of tears gently creases her cheek as she fights to subdue this unexpected emotion. In a clumsy attempt to be compassionate you ask the woman if she would like to talk. She responds quietly, but favorably, and you move to the museum coffee house where you order coffee and your conversation begins.

Over your drinks, you discover that the painting reminded her of her seven-year old daughter who died a year ago from Leukemia. You feel deep sadness for this new friend. In fact, you find yourself choked by emotion and are drawn into reflecting on your own significant losses. An hour or so later you

---

[118] On Religion, Speech #3, pp. 141-161.

conclude your conversation and depart.[119]

This example is meant to illustrate the way in which Schleiermacher's aesthetic insight into religious experience leads out to an intuition of the infinite. Its sufficiency in illustrating Schleiermacher's point is that it shows the way in which art, as a physical object, can connect a person with spiritual ideals. Through the experience, one's consciousness is expanded to incorporate the experiences of another. Through interaction, you realize your interpretation of the painting differed slightly, but it drew both individuals beyond themselves and thus was community-forming in its nature. This is only an illustration, but it is meant to suggest that material objects can awaken spiritual ideals which can, in turn, lead to greater unities of consciousness and community.

Turning to Speech Four, Schleiermacher deals with the role of the religious community in relationship to religious experience. Here, Schleiermacher defends the existence and necessity of the true church. He begins by rejecting the conventional bias against the church and its typical position as the scapegoat of society's problems. His argument is straightforward and basic.

First, it is human nature to gather in groups. Humans are social animals and are drawn naturally to one another. It is also the nature of religion to draw people into groups. Therefore, the existence of religious communities is not innately evil or even bad, but normal and natural. Therefore, one should look for the meaning conveyed by the existence of religious communities and not simply deplore their existence altogether. The world is filled with religious communities because humans and human experiences are such a varied lot.

Second, by drawing people into specific groups, mutual sharing of the religious spirit ensues. Thus, through speaking and hearing one is able to share one's apprehension of the infinite and gain further insight by having others share their own experience of the infinite. Thus, the use of language within a specific context conveys a specific meaning. This context, moreover, can provide further signs producing intuitions of the infinite.

This mutual exchange leads to Schleiermacher's contention that the true church is based on mutual exchange not hierarchy. In this emphasis, he advocates

---

[119] This example is drawn from the author's own life.

a community where true religion is the mutual exchange between equals who have apprehended the infinite. The true church is not the visible church, though he wish that it were. Nevertheless, the true church is a part of the visible church and must always intermingle with it. Thus, the visible church has the essential elements which can build bridges between the individual and the ultimate realm of eternal meaning.

What, then, are the natures of the two communities, the true and the common church? The true church is that legion of people who have experienced a religious intuition of the infinite and are seeking to understand this intuition further. The true church utilizes all finite activities to encourage attention to the infinite and identifies the authenticity of such events according to their ability to catapult the human onto a higher plane for understanding the universe. All finite activities, therefore, are signs. They distill particular realities, but can also lead to realities beyond themselves.

By contrast, the common church is merely a self-perpetuating organization. Here, all people want to take and no one wants to give. No mutual exchange occurs. The preacher is the repository of religion from which everyone else borrows. No one has a real religious life, but only one which is based on appearance. In this church, such finite human activities as the sacraments are used not as signs which facilitate a quest for the infinite, but to reinforce tradition and shackle the human spirit through a mechanistic performance of ritual.

Because of this tendency, Schleiermacher advocates the break up of the state-regulated parish system. In advocating the free association of individuals, Schleiermacher sought to remove the corrupting restraints of finite institutions in order to allow the human spirit, in search of the infinite, to roam freely throughout all finite experiences. Only as humans gathered freely would one be free to apprehend the infinite fully.[120]

The concluding speech, Speech Five, deals even more specifically with the necessary particularity of religious communities. Under the guise of dealing with the subject of religious pluralism, Schleiermacher outlines why the intuition of the infinite must take on various forms within religious communities and why these

---

[120] On Religion, Speech #4, pp. 162-188.

particular forms are still true to the essence of the religious spirit. Because no individual and no single religion can possess the intuition of the infinite fully, human apprehension of the infinite must always take on finite form. Humans are finite; religion is infinite. Therefore, the intuition of the infinite must take on particular form. According to Schleiermacher's case, this means the Christian church.

It is impossible to do otherwise. To evaluate other religions accurately one must have had an intuition of the infinite. If this intuition is not nurtured in a specific community, however, it will gradually fade until it dies. Therefore, every intuition of the infinite draws one into community with others who have also experienced an intuition of the infinite. From within this community one forms signs which signify one's particular understanding of these experiences. From this vantage point, one is able to proceed to evaluate the validity of other claims to experiencing the intuition of the infinite. The key in this speech is Schleiermacher's insistence that humans are finite and everything human, including religious experience, must take on finite form if it is to be capable of being interpreted so that it can provide meaning and endure.

But is every finite form legitimate? Clearly, every form is not legitimate. Yet, Schleiermacher remains ambiguous as to how one distinguishes between legitimate and illegitimate forms of finite religion. He insists on removing all aspects of finite religion which lead to hostility and wars. Yet, he does not endorse other alternatives and he is particularly damning when it comes to any suggestion regarding the inclusion of civil religion or natural religion.

Civil religion is corrupt and natural religion is a fraud. Natural religion is not a religion because there is no apprehension of the infinite that is not nurtured through a community. Natural religion seeks to establish religion on the lowest common denominator and misses the key elements which activate the religious imagination and allow an intuition of the infinite to occur. Civil religion exists only to serve the pragmatic interests of the state. Furthermore, it lacks any substance or power to cultivate one's religious nature and thus has no comprehension of the essence of truly religious people.

Positive religions, by comparison, encourage continual growth of one's religious nature. It is the nature of true religion to be displayed in a concrete, historical form. This is its social context. It is natural for the human to identify the time at which the infinite and finite were united in their own history. This is its personal sign. Together, through interpretation, the personal sign finds meaning within the social context. The interpretation of this experience is not to replace the experience itself, but it is the process by which the fullness of the experience's meaning is carried forward as part of the unifying ideal of an individual's life.

Ultimately, Schleiermacher argues for Christianity's truth because of its accurate understanding that everything holy can be corrupted by its human form. One of the greatest dangers in positive religions is their tendency to institutionalize the original intuition and thereby corrupt its ultimate meaning. Therefore, the constant battle for the human is to probe the frontiers of his or her religious understanding continually. The intuition of the infinite is the beginning of the religious quest; the apprehension of the meaning of this intuition its ultimate ideal.[121]

Schleiermacher's earliest definition of the intuition of the infinite taking on finite form established the dynamic interplay between the individual and the community which would mark the remainder of his work. The foundation for the role of the religious community in interpreting religious experience was laid in these three speeches and helped him recognize the way in which the individual is bound to other individuals through the community. By identifying with a particular religious community, mutual communication among its members could bring out the multiple ways in which religion is experienced and understood. These multiple exchanges are signs which lead to greater understanding in individual religious consciousness.

---

[121] Ibid., Speech #5, pp. 189-223.

47

Individual Religious Experience and the Need for Religious Community

Individual religious experience cannot be sustained apart from the formation of a religious community. Religious communities develop as a result of like minded souls identifying with one another. For religion to be communicated effectively there must be a community solely dedicated to religion and shaped by the distinct form of religious language which it develops.[122]

Religious leaders received sustained and harsh criticism by Schleiermacher's contemporaries. But this criticism indicated a misunderstanding of their role. The preacher is the official representative and the official communicator for the community. The preacher plays a pivotal role in helping shape the religious community through his or her religious discourse.[123] The preacher is an individual, full of religion, who, in turn, communicates this fullness to others.

Schleiermacher's point is to show from the outset that individuals gather together to support and stimulate one another through community and in this support and stimulation religious understanding occurs. He did not deviate from this basic understanding in any subsequent works. In fact, his subsequent works were simply an amplification of this basic insight as he argued for the primary and central role of the religious community in the creation, cultivation, and perpetuation of individual religious consciousness through interpretation.

Through the religious community, one develops social bonds more powerful than political bonds. Although patriotism was a remarkable force among the Germanic peoples, Schleiermacher believed that the love and loyalty one felt for one's religious community was more powerful than any feeling evoked by patriotism. In one telling phrase, Schleiermacher exclaimed,

> ...Do not find fault with them if this *heavenly bond,*
> the most complete result of human fellowship to
> which religion can attain only when it is recognized
> from the highest standpoint in its innermost essence,

---

[122] Ibid., p. 165.
[123] Ibid. This role receives parallel treatment in Wuthnow, Robert Communities of Discourse. Cambridge, MA: Harvard University Press, 1989.

> is of more value to them than
> your earthly political bond,...which is only a forced,
> transitory, provisional work.[124]

These heavenly bonds are universal in their existence, but particular in their manifestation. Eventually, according to Schleiermacher, all religious associations will become one. There will be a blending at a higher level of religious consciousness whereby all legitimate religious expressions will merge. Later, in the Christian Faith, Schleiermacher refines this position to show how Christian religious consciousness is the highest form of religious consciousness. Nevertheless, Schleiermacher views the development of religious consciousness as formed and developed within the general framework of every religious community.

Within the religious community, a unique and distinct form of communication develops. Because religious experience is the experience of the innermost core of humanity common conversation is unable to capture or communicate the power of religious experience adequately.[125] In specific communities, set aside for the specific purpose of communicating the vibrancy of religious experience, a language unique to this domain develops. In espousing the virtues of this distinct form of language, Schleiermacher states,

> a higher choir, as it were, answers the summoning
> voice in a sublime language all its own[126]

In essence, Schleiermacher is presenting the foundation of the notion that religious communities exist to communicate distinct interpretations of specific realities.[127] Whatever else one may expect from them, religious communities must perpetuate as they propagate their specific understanding of experiences interpreted religiously.

For Schleiermacher, every individual religious experience must be

---

[124] Ibid., p. 166.
[125] On Religion, p. 164.
[126] Ibid., p. 166.
[127] Ibid., p. 168.

contextualized within particular religious communities if understanding is to occur. Although experiences interpreted religiously are universal, there is no universal interpretation which encompasses all religious experiences.

Later, in the <u>Christian Faith</u>, Schleiermacher expands his treatment of the way in which religious consciousness differs in kind and degree based on the religious community. But in both his early and mature period, Schleiermacher sees the religious community as being comprised of all people who are religious. Because Schleiermacher believes religious consciousness is developmental and people become aware of their religious needs in different forms and contexts, he does not believe that religious consciousness giving rise to religious community ever includes the entire populace of the human race.

The communal religious consciousness is formed in an individual by the religious communication used within this social context. The formation of communal religious consciousness differs in kind and degree because of the language, culture and tradition in which it is embedded. Such influences must be checked to ensure they do not corrupt the appropriate formation of communal religious consciousness, but in their development of the communal religious consciousness they reflect the fundamental connection which exists between self-consciousness and religious consciousness.

Language and concept are essential for religious understanding. Without concepts one's intuition of the infinite is impossible to understand. In the process of embedding one's intuition of the infinite in conceptual form, however, the majesty of the original intuition is lost. Every conceptual and linguistic embodiment diminishes the purity of one's religious experience. But it is impossible to understand what one has experienced unless it is put into conceptual and linguistic form.[128]

The danger with conceptual and linguistic forms, however, is that people frequently become more attached to the form than the actual experience. As Schleiermacher states, "...instead of elements of religion, they insist on the abstractions about it."[129] In stating this position, Schleiermacher insists that one

---

[128] <u>Ibid.,</u> p. 172.
[129] <u>Ibid.,</u> p. 172.

recognize that concepts and linguistic forms come after the religious experience and are not to replace it.

But this is too one sided. Granted, the institutional embodiment of religion can introduce corrupting influences. But it is this very embodiment of language and concept in communal form which makes understanding and transmitting religious experience possible.

In identifying the nature of the true church, Schleiermacher recognizes the right role of language as noted earlier. For those who have had genuine religious experiences, 'intuitions of the infinite,' there is a specific language used in a specific context which communicates the reality of this ideal. Thus, within a communal context the truly religious communicate fully and, the more one has experiences interpreted religiously, the more one is compelled to communicate these experiences.

This initial excursion into the role of the religious community in the formation of religious consciousness demonstrates the way in which religion, in its pure state, could be corrupted and tarnished by its imperfect embodiment in the world. Still, even in its historic form it has power as a sign to stimulate the interpretive process leading to understanding. The full treatment of this idea occurs within the mature system of the <u>Christian Faith</u> and it is within this document that the way in which particular religious communities form around unifying ideals becomes evident.

The Development of Religious Consciousness through Particular Religious Communities

The development of religious consciousness is fundamentally anchored to a given community of faith. Religious communities mediate between one's understanding of their religious experience and the way in which this understanding of religious experience impacts the rest of their immediate self-consciousness. The Christian religious community is a direct result of the founding of a human community through the immediate influence of Jesus Christ.

Since the church is a particular religious community, it incorporates several other fields into its definition. First, it is a community like other human communities. Thus, philosophical ethics are relevant in establishing a social theory of community. Next, the church is a religious community formed on the basis of the expression of the distinct category of religious piety. Therefore, philosophy of religion is relevant in establishing the unique features of a religious community. Finally, it is a particular religious community in which everything is related to the redemption accomplished by Jesus of Nazareth.[130] Schleiermacher contends that the church exists as a mediating link between the human and divine realms.

As a result, Christian piety arises because of its historical connection through the church with Jesus Christ.[131] Christian piety arises, moreover, to shape a particular form of the sensible self-consciousness. This form reflects the fundamental understanding brought to an interpretation of religious experience which determines the way in which the feeling of absolute dependence takes shape and is understood in the sensible self-consciousness.[132]

The feeling of absolute dependence one experiences, interprets, and understands is related to the form of sensible self-consciousness conditioned by a particular form of the religious community. The sensible self-consciousness, as a co-mingling of the feeling of freedom and the feeling of dependence, differs in the degree to which it presents or understands the feeling of absolute dependence based on the understanding which has developed within the religious community.

Religious communities form because humans have religious experiences they interpret similarly and gather naturally into 'communities of kind' who share these experiences. Fellowship is a natural development arising from a need to relate and share with others who have had similar experiences. Through these relations, individuals are able to gain insight and clarity as their experiences are interpreted within the broader context of a religious community. Only when one goes beyond one's self and takes up facts of other personalities through one's involvement in the community, is one able to express in external form what one

---

[130] Ibid., p. 55, #11.
[131] Ibid., p. 45, #10.1.
[132] Ibid., p. 22, #5.4.

has discovered as an internal reality.[133]   Thus, the community forms a context in which a greater understanding of religious experience develops.

The religious community must develop at every level of social intercourse because a religious community is pivotal for the development of religious consciousness.   Since religion is fundamentally constituted and contextualized within human communities, there is no such thing as a natural religion.   Natural religion, or, a religionless religion, cannot exist because natural religion fails to acknowledge or appreciate the primary role the religious community plays in the formation and perpetuation of one's religious understanding.[134]   Because of this neglect, natural religion fails to encompass the full range of what it means to be human.   The human nature of religious communities is what makes them an essential sign for mediating to an individual religious consciousness a Feeling of Absolute Dependence.

Why Religious Communities Differ

Religious communities differ according to kind and degree.   What Schleiermacher means by this is that whereas every religious community is based on piety, the way in which each religious consciousness is embedded within the community develops at different levels and in different ways based on each community's understanding of the nature and purpose of the religious life.   Every religious communion is related to every other religious community because of its common heritage as an expression of religious piety.   This common origin, however, has failed to restrict the religious consciousness to a singular form or expression.   All religious experiences give rise to religious communities, but not all religious communities understand religious experience in the same way.

The Christian religious community has developed as a result of the influence of the spirit of Christ in shaping the texture of the Christian religious community and its members through his God-consciousness.[135]   The role of

---

[133] Ibid., p. 27, 6.2.
[134] Ibid., p. 30, #6.Postscript.
[135] Ibid., p. 56, #11.4.

Christ in the formation of the Christian religious community is pivotal for understanding the distinctiveness of the Christian religious community as a form of religious consciousness separate from every other religious group. The redemption accomplished in Jesus of Nazareth is the distribution of his God-consciousness through the Christian religious community.

The emergence of Jesus' God-consciousness was not simply a result of a spiritual process within himself, but an entirely new development leading to the start of a new religion.[136] The central truth conveyed by Christ is the recognition that as humans discover their need for redemption as a lack of God-consciousness, or God-forgetfulness, they also become aware of the sole way in which they can satisfy their God-forgetfulness through identity with the God-consciousness of Jesus Christ. The only way to experience the influence of the God-consciousness of Jesus Christ is through the church.

Every religious community is a manifestation of religious consciousness. Christianity is the highest form of religious consciousness and the Christian religious community is the highest expression of the highest form of communal religious consciousness. Every other form of religious community and religious consciousness is only preparatory for assimilation into the Christian religious community and the Christian religious consciousness.

Christianity is the highest form of religious consciousness because it captures the essence of the religious spirit and best expresses this spirit in finite form. Because Christianity advocates continuous growth as the nature of all true religions and because Christianity, of all positive religions, best captures this dynamic it is supreme.

Christianity, moreover, is the highest religion because of the inadequate way in which other religions have developed around a single, centering intuition. Natural Religion, Personalism, Pantheism and Polytheism are all inadequate because they fail to offer any definitive evidence of a centering intuition. Judaism, although elevated above these and other forms of false religion, remains inadequate because it diminishes the necessity of an intuition of the infinite and perpetuates a system of rewards and punishments unacceptable to an enlightened

---

[136] Ibid., p. 63, 13.1.

human.

Christianity, by contrast, offers the highest and most original intuition which is worthy of a developed human consciousness. Christianity's intuition is not confined to a specific community nor a particular place, but circles the globe inspiring all who encounter it to an intuition of the infinite. Christianity, moreover, offers the highest centering intuition because it commences with the intuition of Jesus Christ. Because Jesus' intuition came without social or civil support, but introduced an original intuition into the religious universe it is reliable. Because Jesus advocated that his intuition was the commencement and not the conclusion of a higher religious consciousness his intuition is to be followed, emulated and embraced. In the example of Jesus Christ the way in which the highest ideal of how the religious intuition both enters finite form and moves beyond all finite forms to greater apprehension of this spirit is captured. In this dual activity the genius and superiority of Christianity is found.

The Religious Use of Language

Religious communions are shaped by and, in turn, shape the use of language. The use of language in the religious sphere is a unique use of language. As such, dogmatic propositions, as expressions of religious language, are meaningful only within the context in which they are formed and retain their relevance and meaning only within this context. Religious language is a unique use of language and is used both to express and to form individual and religious consciousness.[137]

Religious language allows religious ideas and understandings to be formed and expressed. Religious ideas distilled as doctrines already express the formation of a Christian religious consciousness. This religious consciousness is formed in community and expressed as a result of the language and symbol structure of the community.[138] These ideas, moreover, are unique to the Christian community. Each form of religious piety giving rise to a religious community

---

[137] Ibid., p. 81, #16.Postscript.
[138] Ibid., p. 94, #20.

understands the formation of religious consciousness in a unique way. The distinctive element of Christian religious consciousness is that every form of religious expression is anchored in some way to the person and work of Jesus Christ.[139]

Schleiermacher is careful to note that in his explication of how Christian religious community forms he is not explaining how all religious communities form. While the formation of all religious communities is based on the feeling of piety, there is no reason to assume they form in the exact same way.[140] Christian religious community develops because of the unique influence of Jesus Christ. This unique influence is carried forward through the religious community.

Subsequent to Christ's reported ascension into heaven, the living contact every member of the Christian religious community has enjoyed with Jesus has been mediated through the activity of the church. What Schleiermacher demonstrates is the fact that the human as human, can only experience God in forms perceptible to the human. Thus, the only way to experience God is through forms inherent to human nature. Since the human is fundamentally social, the experience of God through the social sign of the church is primary.

The Influence of Jesus

Without identifying with the Christian church it is impossible to come into living contact with Jesus Christ. If one does not come into living contact with Jesus it is impossible to develop a Christian religious consciousness. The church is essential for the mediation of Christ's presence because it shows the manner in which Christ is mediated through time and space in order to have a continuing influence in the life of each new generation of individuals shaped and influenced by a Christian religious consciousness.

The influence of Jesus' God-consciousness is mediated through Christian religious consciousness and is experienced in both personal consciousness and communal consciousness. The experience within personal consciousness is that

---

[139] Ibid., p. 132, #32.2.
[140] Ibid., p. 360, #87.3.

the individual receives the impact of Jesus' sinless perfection as both a corporate act of sin and a perfect removal of the misery caused by sin.[141]   The experience within communal consciousness is that in all these different expressions of the Christian church, as sinful as they may be, there exists the common consciousness of Christ's God-consciousness which can be mediated to each individual member.

Jesus exemplifies in his own life the example of the conjoining of the supernatural and the natural as one. The supernatural in Jesus is the explanation for the origin of his perfect God-consciousness originating outside human nature, while its expression through the Christian church is an expression of the way in which it takes form as human receptivity of the potency of God-consciousness, allowing the supernatural to become a natural fact of history. Thus, the Christian church exists as the mediating link in which one can interpret his or her religious experience in relation to God. The church is a sign-signifier that contains the potency to elevate a person beyond the contingent, disjointed experiences of his or her personal life and bring them into contact with a realm where an overarching ideal can unite these experiences in a meaningful whole.

The coherence of the Christian religious consciousness clusters around the universal consciousness of the redeemer and his act of redemption for the world. Thus, the entrance of Christ is the one event which forms the religious community and brings the Christian religious consciousness into existence and expression.[142]

The necessity of the Christian religious community is to counter the sinful influence of the world.[143]   Since the human is social and since the goal of the Christian life is the blessedness of full participation in the God-consciousness of Jesus, this blessedness can only be communicated through the development of a new religious community.[144] Since the corporate life of the church is formed out of the corporate life of the world, there is always a possibility of the incursion of sin on the life of the church as the body of Christ. But this new life can counter the sinful influence originating in the corporate life of the world.

The new life from which this community springs, is the life of the

---

[141] Ibid., p. 364.
[142] Ibid., p. 373.
[143] Ibid., p. 387.
[144] Ibid., p. 358, #87.

Redeemer. Schleiermacher writes,

> ...the new life of each individual springs from that of the community, while the life of the community springs from no other individual life than that of the Redeemer...[145]

Schleiermacher extends this point by noting that the formation of an external fellowship and an internal fellowship has distinguished the corporate life of the Christian religious community. The formation of the first Christian fellowship, moreover, is difficult to discern and is frankly unimportant. The spiritual influence of Christ carries by nature a community-forming principle within it. Therefore, to be impacted by this community and to experience the God-consciousness of Christ is to be drawn into the Christian religious community.[146]

Those who do not share a Christian religious consciousness cannot understand this perspective. They do not see that without the community no redemptive activity can occur in the life of the individual.[147] Thus, Schleiermacher advocates that without the church it is impossible to attain either one's understanding of a need for salvation or of Christ's provision for this need.

The Christian church continues to develop as individuals are incorporated into association with the God-consciousness of Jesus Christ.[148] This inaugurates a new life in which one comes to identify more and more with the Christian religious community and less and less with the world. This development corresponds to the increasing development of one's God-consciousness in the world.

---

[145] Ibid., p. 525, #113.
[146] Pannenberg writes that Schleiermacher's point in establishing the role of the church was a foreshadowing of the coming kingdom of God in origin, existence, and completion. Pannenberg, Wolfhart. Ethics. Translated by Keith Crim. Philadelphia: Westminster Press, 1981.
[147] Ibid., p. 527.
[148] Ibid., p. 529

58

The Role of Preaching

The church, moreover, provides the context in which the power of preaching can make an impact on those who have inaugurated this new life and have identified themselves as part of the Christian religious community. Thus, the individual becomes not only an independent personality specifically influenced by the potency of Christ's God-consciousness, but a representative of every other individual who enters into the Christian church because of the universal need and desire for the redemption accomplished by Jesus of Nazareth.[149]

The preaching activity of Christ helped to form the first Christian community. This religious fellowship grew out of the individuals whose God-consciousness was awakened by Christ's life and ministry. Since Christ's main activity was preaching, every subsequent generation is drawn into an awareness of Christ's God-consciousness through preaching. But preaching only brings partial success. Even though all hear equally, not all respond equally. An uneven response to the same sermon frequently occurs and seems to indicate that some are at a more advanced developmental state and can, therefore, respond to the significance of the words delivered in preaching. Others, however, remain in a state of arrested God-consciousness and have not yet developed to the level at which they can respond in fullness to the prompting of Christ's God-consciousness communicated through preaching.[150]

Schleiermacher recognized the power of preaching to influence the hearts and minds of his congregation in their Christian life. Preaching is a perfect example of the way in which a human form, speech, can be used to mediate a divine reality. A central concern in preaching is to convey a sense of God's will that is understandable and appropriately addressed to the present concerns of one's religious community. Schleiermacher expressed this interest by stating,

> ...let our goal be that the community of the Lord
> lives in each, of the Lord for whom we are all to

---

[149] Ibid., p. 531.
[150] Ibid., p. 534.

live as a matter of honor and of joy and for whom, together with his and our heavenly Father, be the honor and praise by his Holy Spirit.[151]

Schleiermacher also recognized the power of preaching to influence the hearts and minds of his congregation in their civic life. It is well known that Schleiermacher combined his responsibilities as a professor with a posterity at Trinity Church, Berlin.[152] During a significant portion of this period, both Prussia and Schleiermacher endured incredible hardship as Napoleon paraded back and forth across their land.[153] Schleiermacher used his pulpit to critique the enemy, frequently mixing patriotic rhetoric with theological discourse.[154] Elsewhere, he used his pulpit to pursue the unification of the German states, addressing the spiritual needs of the Prussian people and promoting the increasing separation of church and state.

Because preaching is so critical for the perpetuation of Christ's God-consciousness mediated through the church, it is only natural that a permanent institution would emerge to ensure the permanence of this communication. The creation of the institution of the organized church or religious community helps the individual move from a sin state to outer fellowship with the God-consciousness of Christ. Likewise, the individual moves from outer fellowship into the inner circle where intimacy with and understanding of the potency of Christ's God-consciousness is experienced.[155]

Thus, from the single individual Jesus Christ, emerges a multitude of

---

[151] Schleiermacher, F.D.E. The Christian Household: A Sermonic Treatise. Translated from 1820, 1826 editions by Dietrich Seidel and Terrence N. Tice. Lewiston, NY: Edwin Mellen Press, 1991, p. xxxvii.

[152] Redeker, Martin. Friedrich Schleiermacher: Life and Thought. Translated by John Wallhausser. Philadelphia: Fortress Press, 1973, p. 26.

[153] Dawson, Jerry F. Friedrich Schleiermacher: The Evolution of a Nationalist. Austin, TX: University of Texas Press, 1966.

[154] Selected Sermons of Schleiermacher. Translated by Mary F. Wilson. New York: Funk and Wagnalls, 1860, pp. 67-78. "A Nation's Duty in a War for Freedom," preached March 28, 1813. Another significant sermon was preached on October 18,1818, on the anniversary of the battle of Leipzig, entitled, "Rejoicing Before God," (Wilson text, p. 183 ff.) which is also reflective of Schleiermacher's patriotic feelings.

[155] Ibid., p. 539.

people influenced by his preaching to form an organic whole.[156]   Within this
organic whole a common spirit develops which allows every regenerate individual
to become an indispensable part of the Christian religious community. The way
in which the Church comprehends and acts is meant to preserve and perpetuate
the original communication and activity of the life of Jesus.[157]

The Christian community must develop over time. As it develops, it will
produce a 'Gemeinsinn,' a 'shared sense of things,' or a 'Gemeingeist,' a
'common spirit.'[158]   That is, it will develop heavenly bonds which mediate
between one's contingent experiences in the world and one's contact with the
ultimate level of reality wherein these experiences are infused with meaning and
make sense.

The Role of the Holy Spirit/Common Spirit

Eventually, this common spirit became synonymous with the Holy Spirit.
Schleiermacher has been roundly criticized for seeming to drop off the third
person of the Trinity and for equating the spirit of Christ with the common spirit
of the Church.[159]   In Schleiermacher's system, the Holy Spirit is understood as
that which produces and symbolizes the vital unity of the Christian fellowship.
The Holy Spirit is the divine influence originating in Christ and continuing
through history as the common spirit of the church.[160]

The Holy Spirit, moreover, is the spirit that leads every individual element
into submission to the corporate life of the community. If there were no common
spirit producing this spirit in the individual members there would be no true
common or corporate life. Through this common spirit, moreover, individual
differences are modified as a common feeling and a common spirit develops
among all members and participants.[161]   Thus, the Holy Spirit acts to create 'felt

---

[156] Ibid., p. 562.
[157] Ibid., p. 579.
[158] Ibid., p. 142, 169.
[159] Hodgson, Peter.   The Formation of Historical Theology. New York: Harper and Row, 1966, p. 112.
[160] Schleiermacher, F. The Christian Faith, p. 535.
[161] Schleiermacher, F. The Christian Faith, p. 542.

unities,' or bonds, which connect the individual with the communal realm beyond the individual.

The drive to become "one" in community is seen in the continuing influence of the Holy Spirit on the lives of the members of the Church. The Holy Spirit, as the common spirit of the church, creates a common spirit in each member of the church. As such, the Holy Spirit helps individuals develop a consciousness of being members of the whole, as it develops within each individual a consciousness of his or her need to be a part of the whole.[162]

Schleiermacher is careful to distinguish the Holy Spirit from his explication of the concept of race consciousness. The Holy Spirit is the spirit which is drawing not only all members of the Christian church into unity, but also all members of every other religion into Christianity. Thus, the Holy Spirit is distinct from race consciousness because through the Holy Spirit an individual's religious consciousness develops in relation to communal religious consciousness. By contrast, race consciousness works on the sensible self-consciousness, but is unable to develop the sense of personal religious consciousness which leads one to find redemption. The difference is race consciousness is based on an awareness which recognizes only the natural plane. One does not need a bond-building, interpretive insight. The other, the common spirit, or the Holy Spirit, is a recognition that human elements can elevate the natural spirit to divine realities.

According to Schleiermacher, the Holy Spirit did not come into full religious consciousness until after the ascension of Christ. As such, the Holy Spirit became the vitalizing power of the Christian religious community. As the vitalizing power of the church, the Holy Spirit communicated the God-consciousness of Jesus through the fundamental structures of human life; between a living receptivity and a free spontaneous activity.[163] In fact, without the active agent of the Holy Spirit, it would be impossible to apprehend Christ correctly.

The Holy Spirit is critical for the perpetuation of Christ's God-consciousness, for without the vitalizing influence of the Holy Spirit, it would be impossible to transmit Christ's God-consciousness to subsequent generations. If

---

[162] Ibid., p. 563.
[163] Ibid., p. 566, #122.

the followers of an individual do not find a spiritual bond to replace the loyalty they have felt for their master they will disperse and the community they were a part of will be short lived. Conversely, if a common spirit develops as a result of the impact of an individual leader, this common spirit, more than the life of the individual leader, becomes the sustaining force for preserving the community.[164] In other words, the individual who founds the community does so by helping his adherents come in contact with the common spirit, which is universal.

As a result, subsequent to Christ's departure, the first disciples were changed from being receptive to the influence of Christ to producing, through spontaneous activity, the spirit of Christ through the ministry of the Christian religious community. It is because Christ's direct influence is a community forming influence that the disciples gathered together into the first explicit Christian religious community wherein they expressed the earliest understanding of the Christian religious consciousness. For subsequent generations, it is Christ's influence mediated through the Christian religious community that reproduces the Christian religious consciousness.

Schleiermacher defines the role of the Holy Spirit in explicit terms when he states that the Holy Spirit is the mediating link between the divine and the human. Schleiermacher writes,

> ...The Holy Spirit is the union of the Divine Essence
> with human nature in the form of the common spirit
> animating the life in common of believers.[165]

Schleiermacher's explicit concern in identifying the Holy Spirit in this way and ascribing to the Holy Spirit this role is to show that the Holy Spirit is the central vitalizing force drawing the entire Christian religious community together. The significance of this is that although Schleiermacher will clearly ascribe universality to the Holy Spirit, this universality is clearly restricted to the variety of manifestations of the Christian religious community spread throughout the

---

[164] Ibid., p. 568.
[165] Ibid., p. 569, #123.

world.[166]

The Holy Spirit is manifested through human speech and significant action. Thus, through human forms only those who are first influenced by the God-consciousness of Christ are fit to serve as transmitters of this God-consciousness to subsequent individuals. When the Holy Spirit is operant, the influence of Christ's God-consciousness works on one's sensible self-consciousness to raise it to greater awareness and to move one towards the full development of religious consciousness.

It is impossible to enter the true church without the influence of the Holy Spirit. In fact, what seems to distinguish those in the outer circle of the Christian church from those who are members of the true church is the degree to which they have been influenced by the consciousness of Jesus Christ mediated by the communal consciousness of the Holy Spirit.[167]

To be a member of the Christian church is to be within the sphere of influence of the consciousness of Christ. Therefore, to be influenced by the Holy Spirit and to place oneself within the sphere of influence of the Christian religious consciousness is the same thing. After Christ's ascension into heaven it is impossible to have living fellowship with Him unless we have contact with the Christian religious community.

When Paul defined the Christian religious community as the body of Christ, this was more than an analogy. This was literally true. The church as the body of Christ became the only empirical means of establishing a relationship with the consciousness of Christ.

Through the activity of the Holy Spirit the ministry of redemption is continued and extended in the church. Since the specific goal of the Christian religious consciousness is to realize redemption in every individual, the activity of the Holy Spirit becomes universal wherever the universal need for redemption is recognized and desired. Although the initial outpouring of the Holy Spirit on the day of Pentecost bears the mark of the miraculous there is no reason to be constrained to this view. Clearly, the later communications of the Holy Spirit,

---

[166] Ibid., p. 571.
[167] Ibid., p. 574.

particularly through the preaching ministry of the church, are identical in influence and effect as the initial outpouring on the day of Pentecost.[168]

Since the human is created as a social being he or she needs a social context in order to develop human consciousness fully. If one fails to identify with a community then one's self-development will be arrested. Likewise, if one fails to identify with a religious community one's religious development will be arrested.[169] Such identification of an individual with a community allows one to develop fully and to express one's Christian religious consciousness fully. In addition, it allows an individual to recognize the fundamental role the church plays in mediating the reality of Christ and his God-consciousness to every member of the Christian church.[170]

The uniqueness of the Christian religious consciousness is amplified by Schleiermacher through his emphasis that although Judaism and Christianity both have the feeling of absolute dependence present in their religious understandings, the feeling of absolute dependence is shaped differently because of the differences in the respective religious communities. Thus, the Christian religious community modifies the feeling of absolute dependence to become a teleological impulse to thought and action.

Within the Christian religious community, moreover, the individual is affected by the whole community and understands him or herself only in relation to this whole community.[171] The church is a unique embodiment of community. It is distinct unto itself and differs from the general world as a closed community. Within this closed community, language takes on specific uses and is instrumental in the formation of a unique expression of Christian religious consciousness.[172]

Thus, Christian ethics, for example, as a specific form of ethics, is prescriptive only for the Christian church. And, within the Christian church, only pertinent for Protestant Christians since this is the specific group to whom

---

[168] Ibid., p. 578.
[169] Schleiermacher, F. The Christian Household, p. 170, 221, 225.
[170] ibid., p. 171,177, 227.
[171] Schleiermacher, F. Introduction to Christian Ethics. Translated from notes, Winter semester, 1826/27, by John C. Shelley. Nashville: Abingdon Press, 1989
[172] Ibid., p. 38.

Schleiermacher is addressing his work. Christian ethics, as the ethics of a particular expression of community, is grounded in the revelation of God in Jesus Christ and valid for the Christian religious community.

But there is no universal Christian ethic which binds the church for all time. The universal element in Christian ethics is that all ethical teachings reflect the influence of the person and work of Jesus. Every specific expression of this ethic will vary based on the relationship the church enjoys with the state.[173] The two focal points of Christian ethics are a doctrine of Christ as the pattern of life and a doctrine of the Holy Spirit as the power from which the Christian life arises.

The distinguishing mark between Roman Catholic and Protestant Christian religious consciousness, moreover, is found in the authority given to church teaching and tradition in the former and one's individual conscience instructed by Scripture in the latter. For Roman Catholics, Christian ethics is mediated by the historic authority residing in the teaching of the church and the tradition of interpreting this tradition. For Protestants, Christian ethics is mediated by the obedience of one's personal conscience instructed by Scripture. The synthesizing agent in both perspectives is the foundation established by the Christian church as the medium through which either history and tradition or conscience and Scripture derive their authority over an individual member within a specific Christian religious community.[174]

The Role of Doctrines in the Formation of
Christian Religious Consciousness

In expressing his philosophy of the Christian religious community, Schleiermacher deliberately combined his ecclesiastical interests with his concern for scientific expression of these interests. In this way, Schleiermacher demonstrates that religious interests must build through systems, or paradigms, which communicate in forms plausible to human reason. In Brief Outline of Theology As a Field of Study, for example, Schleiermacher identifies his ideal

---

[173] Ibid., p. 82.
[174] Ibid., p. 93.

church leader as a 'prince of the church' in whom both a religious interest and a scientific spirit were joined in the highest degrees and with the finest balance for the purpose of theoretical and practical activity alike.[175] Thus, the leader of the church becomes the embodiment of Schleiermacher's ideal of a human entity mediating between a divine realm and other human realities.

This ideal expresses Schleiermacher's understanding of the dual relationship which must exist between scientific conception and historical embodiment. The two work side by side, not in opposition or ignorance of one another. The value of the scientific conception of doctrine is the definiteness of their concepts and the way in which a scientific conception helps to identify systematic interconnections.[176]

Doctrines are expressions of the religious self-consciousness. As a result of the formation of doctrine, the Christian religious consciousness is able to interpret specific religious experiences in order to articulate the meaning of these experiences to each individual. The doctrines which articulate Christian religious experience, moreover, are regulated by the same laws of conception and synthesis which regulate all speech.

In addition, Christian doctrines direct our attention to others who share similar experiences and a kindred spirit.[177] Doctrines are the scientific formulation of religious experience which influences the shape of the ecclesiastical community. Thus, the Christian community becomes a corporate individual with a personality of its own in that all aspects of doctrine either promote health or introduce decay.

Within Christian doctrine, moreover, all doctrines are either "descriptions of human states," "conceptions of divine attributes and modes of action," or "statements regarding the constitution of the world."[178] All three exist alongside of one another in reciprocal interaction and their influence on one another does

---

[175] Schleiermacher, Friedrich. Brief Outline of Theology as A Field of Study. Translation of the 1811 and 1830 editions, with Essays and Notes, by Terrence N. Tice. (Lewiston, NY: Edwin Mellen Press, 1990).
[176] Ibid., #17, 1,2.
[177] The Christian Faith, p. 84, #17.
[178] Ibid., p. 125, #30.

not always appear as a seamless garment. Because they have developed over time, particularly as the church confronted different obstacles in its growth and development, the reliability of doctrine has come to be based on its appeal to historic confessional documents of the church or to New Testament Scriptures. In addition, these doctrines must demonstrate the way in which new developments of each doctrine are continuous with the past understandings of these doctrines.[179]

Christian doctrine must not be contrary to reason. In fact, because Christian doctrine is a combination of a systematic approach to religion and an ecclesial concern for the transmission and perpetuation of Christian faith, they must be reasonable in order to be apprehended. Through the combination of human thought and speech in the creation and cultivation of religious symbols, signs, and acts, religious doctrine is made reasonable. This combination allows for a vast range of expressions which comprise the religious consciousness.[180]

In expressing Christian doctrine, moreover, two primary forms of expression are utilized: the poetic form and the rhetorical form. The poetic form is typified as originating from within and is descriptive of the state or experience as we have come to understand it. The rhetorical type, by contrast, originates from without and is meant to express and stimulate the understanding of another.[181]

These dual uses of expression reflect the dual purpose of doctrine, expressing both an ecclesiastical concern and a scientific value. The ecclesial concern of doctrine is to establish the pattern and understanding for the Christian religious community. Christian doctrine is typified by its reference to Jesus Christ. As such, in basing all of its reference to Jesus Christ, it functions to express a particular ideal for a religious community in the same way a constitution functions to embody and express an ideal for a state. The scientific value, by contrast, attempts to provide definiteness to concepts and to demonstrate the interaction and connection each part has with the whole. Together, the ecclesial and scientific value of doctrine reflects the coherent and contingent elements of

---

[179] Ibid., p. 127, #31.
[180] Ibid., p. 77, #15.1.
[181] Ibid., p. 79, #16.

Christian religious consciousness.[182]

Again, doctrine is established to serve a specific purpose within the Christian religious community. The purpose of doctrine is to give structure and meaning to the Christian religious affections set forth in speech. Doctrine is to serve the cause of transmitting the Christian religious consciousness through the growth and development of the church. All doctrines must be taken from the religious experiences of people who call themselves Christian.[183] Since all Christian doctrine originates from the self-proclamation of Jesus, an adequate understanding of his self-proclamation must arise from historical theology and Scripture.[184]

The relation between doctrine and Scripture is critical for the life and sustenance of the Church. Scripture is a form of doctrine in that Scripture itself is an expression of religious emotions set forth in speech. Thus, Dogmatic Theology and Biblical Exegesis proceed on the same basic premises. As a result, it is critically important to demonstrate the interconnection between the various forms of dogmatics which will develop.

Scriptural Dogmatics is built by emphasizing scripture over the confessional statements of the Church. Scientific Dogmatics works to provide orderly flow and structure to all expressions of Christian doctrines. As such, it works to provide a coherent framework for every expression of dogmatics. Symbolic Dogmatics, by contrast, is the form of dogmatics which places primary emphasis on the confessional statements of the church over Scripture. The goal, according to Schleiermacher, is to provide the context within which all three approaches to dogmatics can work in relation to one another.[185]

In providing this context, moreover, Schleiermacher envisions that the religious community, as the embodiment of communal religious consciousness, will work to perpetuate the distinctive religious consciousness of its community and will strengthen this embodiment in the future.[186] The religious community

---

[182] Ibid., p. 84, #17.
[183] Ibid., p. 265, #64.
[184] Ibid., p. 93.
[185] Ibid., p. 117, #27.
[186] Brief Outline, p. 67, #177.

provides the context within which the outer form of religious experience and the inner reality of this experience can be continuous with the past, interpreted in the present as it is transported into the future.

The on-going revelation of God in Christ is mediated by the Holy Spirit within and through the Church.[187]   Although we enter the Christian religious community voluntarily,[188] the communal consciousness of the community exerts an involuntary influence on us in which the community-forming consciousness of Christ draws us into relationship with one another.[189]   Through incorporation into and participation within the Christian religious community, the communication of the redemptive life-giving principle of Christianity occurs.   In essence, such incorporation, is, for Schleiermacher, the redemptive influence of Jesus Christ on each individual member.   As the communal consciousness expressed by Christ comes to live within each one of us it also expands an individual's perspective and provides the opportunity for the Christian religious consciousness to originate and develop.

In essence, the purpose of doctrine is to provide the Christian religious community with the guidance it requires in order to preserve and transmit the Christian religious consciousness which originates in Jesus Christ.   As such, it reflects the influence of many sociological factors in its origin and existence. Doctrine, thus, works to preserve Christianity's connection with the inherent nature of all religious communities while recognizing the way in which the unique understandings communicated by Christianity can adjust to the specific realities of every historic and contingent age.

The Role of Tradition and Scripture

Along with doctrine, Schleiermacher acknowledges the important function of tradition in the preservation and perpetuation of Christian religious consciousness.   Tradition, in the Christian religious community, functions in a

---

[187] Tice, vol. 2, p. 384.
[188] On Religion, p. 17.
[189] Christian Faith, pp. 432-433.

similar vein to doctrine: both work to provide the historical continuity between Jesus' original self-communication and the present life of the Christian religious community. Tradition, like doctrine, was originally one and the same with Christ's proclamation of His own God-consciousness as recorded in the Gospels.[190]

A vital expression of Christian tradition is captured in the preaching of the first Apostles who, in speaking of their experience of God through Christ, expressed for the first time the continuity of Christ's God-consciousness into the next generation. In elevating tradition to the role of primary and not secondary status, moreover, Schleiermacher countered a dangerous trend in Protestantism which had neglected the role of tradition in its exclusive focus on Scripture. As a result, the Protestant expression of the church as anchored to Scripture has overlooked the way in which Scripture originated and continues to function within the life of the church.

Thus, Scripture, as an expression of tradition, provides the foundation for the creation of a Christian religious community. The authority of Scripture, moreover, is anchored to the Christian religious community and has no authority outside the Christian religious community. Thus, the authority of Scripture is not self-evident, but contingent on the formation of faith which gives rise to the religious community. As such, the Scriptures become normative not only because they are the first expressions of Christian faith, but also because they are normative for all subsequent generations who must assess the validity of their religious affections in relationship to the original expressions of the Christian faith.

Although Schleiermacher reflects many parallels with several Roman Catholic theologians of his time, his treatment of Scripture and tradition differs from the Roman Catholics on the premise that Scripture has *superior* normative value over tradition. Its superior normative value, moreover, is based not simply on its origin in the Apostolic period, but in capturing the essence of the Christian religious consciousness in its recording of Jesus' person and work in the

---

[190] Ibid., p. 588.

preaching of the first apostles.[191] Thus, the essence of tradition is in the preservation and perpetuation of Scripture and in Scripture's distillation of the God-consciousness of Jesus Christ.

In presenting the role of Scripture, tradition, and the relation of Scripture and tradition, Schleiermacher also attempts to emphasize that no part of New Testament Scripture should take precedence over any other part. Specifically, he was concerned to restrict the elevation of any specific individual over the corporate checks and balances which one encounters in interpreting Scripture. In articulating this point, Schleiermacher emphasized that,

> ...each Apostle found not only his complement but his corrective in one of the other Apostles.[192]

Ultimately, the Scriptures are normative because through them the spirit enables one to experience the power of Christ and to be drawn into the blessedness of Christ's God-consciousness.[193]

This emphasis reflects Schleiermacher's fundamental tenet that the saving influence of Christ which gave rise to the first Christian community continues through history, stimulating the potency of God-consciousness in each subsequent generation. This consciousness, moreover, is a result of the combination of religious symbols, acts, teachings, writings and proclamations in the cultivation of the Christian religious consciousness in the members of its community.[194]

This must be the case, otherwise it would be impossible to argue for a unique understanding of the Christian religious consciousness. The influence of the God-consciousness of Christ through the church establishes the basis upon which all subsequent understandings can be considered Christian. This forms the normative principle of what it means to be a Christian and prevents the dissolution of the community and the elevation of individual enlightenment in exclusion to the mediating necessity of the community.

---

[191] Ibid., p. 590.
[192] I bid., p. 596.
[193] Ibid., p. 431ff., 479, 488, 499, 504, 509, 510, 631.
[194] On Religion, p. 108.

Without the Christian community it is impossible to experience the God-consciousness of Christ. Without experiencing the God-consciousness of Christ it is impossible to be a Christian. Without becoming a Christian it is impossible to preserve the uniqueness of the Christian religious fellowship. Without the Christian religious fellowship it is impossible to establish the difference in kind and degree between different understandings and manifestations of the communal nature of religious consciousness.[195]

In 1910, Ernst Troeltsch highlighted this fact in a major essay on Schleiermacher's conception of the church. In commenting on Schleiermacher's notion of the church, Troeltsch observed that Schleiermacher's Christian Faith is virtually incomprehensible unless one considers it in light of his "sociology of the religious consciousness."[196] Troeltsch observes that,

> Schleiermacher employs the concept of the church in a new way: it is neither church nor sect, but rather a new sociological conceptual formation in the realm of religious communal existence.[197]

Troeltsch expands this observation by noting that Schleiermacher developed an alternative to his church-sect distinction which was more than his 'spiritualist' or 'mystic' third option which lacked any sociological principle of organization. Here, in the Christian Faith, Schleiermacher blended the 'church-type' and the 'sect-type' into an organic conception of community in which the church is constituted by the spirit of Christ and is formed by the living connection of the members with the head, which is Christ.

As a result, the church was neither a voluntary organization nor a miraculous institution continuing the incarnation, but an organic community formed by the historic reality of Jesus Christ and flowing forward across time through this historic reality. Troeltsch amplifies this point by noting,

---

[195] Ibid., p. 492.

[196] Troeltsch, Ernst. "Schleiermacher und die Kirche," p. 27, Friedrich Naumann, et. al. Berlin-Schoneberg: Buchverlag der Hilfe, 1910. This point is also highlighted in Wyman, Walter E. Jr. The Concept of Glaubenslehre: Ernst Troeltsch and the Theological Heritage of Schleiermacher. Chico, CA: Scholars Press, 1983, p. 114.

[197] Ibid., p. 30.

> Schleiermacher's ideas...introduce a new concept related to modern organic ideas about the nature of community. A common spirit (Gemeingeist) working forth and witnessing forth from a central point brings forth the individuals, binds and ties them together, gives them the possession of all tradition and grace, independent of their own willing and doing. However, the same common spirit arouses them to the liveliest and most active common activity and the right development of the individual, so that in this work the inherited total spirit transforms itself into one's own possession and into living individual deed.[198]

It is through the religious community that the grace of Christ is communicated in a way which produces the desired redemption as the central feature of Christian religious consciousness. Schleiermacher is particularly sensitive to the dynamic of how Christ's sinless perfection is communicated across time to each new generation of Christians.[199] The form of this communication was the personal influence of Jesus' God-consciousness arousing a consciousness of sin and a longing for transformation through grace.[200] The uniqueness of Christ's God-consciousness is the fullness with which he could love God and the way his entire consciousness was shaped by this love of God.[201]

The communication of Jesus' God-consciousness which mediates grace and redemption is not merely an example or an exemplary witness. This would deny the internal effect of Christ in us and the ability to embrace fully the redemptive influence of Christ. But our ability to be influenced by Christ is still his influence on us and not simply our willful ascription of effect to his life.

This communication of both an external example and an internal effect forms the polarities within which Schleiermacher elevates the religious community as the external mediating agent of Christ's internal mediating effect.[202]

---

[198] Ibid., p. 37.
[199] Christian Faith, #88.
[200] Ibid., #88.2.
[201] Ibid., #104.3.
[202] Schleiermacher, F. The Christian Faith. #101.2. Also, Boyd, George, "The Medium is the Message: A Revisionist Reading of Augustine's Experience of Grace According to

The Christian religious community, or church, is the new corporate life, separated from the rest of society, for the mediation of this expression of Jesus' God-consciousness. As a result of the Christian religious community, the grace of Christ, which mediates redemption, is communicated to the members who have joined the community.

Royce enlarges Schleiermacher's treatment of the religious community to demonstrate the religious nature of all true communities. This treatment and extension will now follow.

Schleiermacher and McLuhan," <u>Anglican Theological Review.</u> Evanston, IL: Seabury-Western Theological Seminary, vol. 56,1974, pp. 189-200.

Chapter Five

The Religious Nature of the Community in Royce

The Overarching Concerns

Royce defends his argument for the church as the body of Christ by reminding his readers that the idea for formulating the doctrine of the person of Christ in this way is not new.[203]   But the church, as the body of Christ, must be exchanged for new currency in order for this insight to be of any value to the modern mentality. The significance of this emphasis, therefore, receives new meaning through a new interpretation of the religious nature of all true communities.[204]

Since the true nature of communities is loyalty mediated through the process of interpretation, an interpretation of Christian community teaches us to hope for the day when the spirit of the community of Christianity will incorporate all of humanity into its Beloved Community.[205] As the body of Christ, the church is both the visible embodiment and the repository of the invisible ideal. As such, the church is the form of the community in which it both preserves the tools necessary for interpretation and the spirit which stimulates all ongoing interpretation.

By defining the community as the body of Christ, Royce tries to demonstrate the inherent social nature of reality. By drawing upon this Pauline metaphor, Royce wants to demonstrate how the Christ-spirit is carried forth in the time-process and provides for each new mind set the context in which the currency of religious ideas can be exchanged. Reality is social. We do not exist as the unencumbered self of the Enlightenment ideal. The community constitutes the fundamental categories of all reality.[206]

---

[203] Royce, J. The Problem of Christianity, vol. II, p. 339.
[204] Royce, J. The Problem of Christianity, vol. I, p. 157.
[205] Royce, J. The Problem of Christianity, vol. II, p. 219.
[206] Ibid., p. 281.

76

As a result, we are beckoned to love this community as an expression of our loyalty. Loyalty, moreover, is the expression of our intentionality of consciousness. This intentionality of consciousness is a manifestation of our individual reason grasping the fundamental nature of reality and our individual will voluntarily aligning our consciousness with the true nature of reality. This ideal is never fully embodied, but only hoped for. On earth, the 'Beloved Community' will never be realized fully. Nevertheless, only within the context of community can one glimpse the real nature of the divine life.[207]

In defining the nature of the community, Royce is careful to note that a community is not merely a collection of individuals.[208] A community, in contrast to a collection of individuals, is based on a union of individuals conscious of their shared commitment both to a common goal in the future and a common understanding of their past.[209] A community, moreover, is a living organism which grows and decays. It has a specific nature reflected in its traditions, rituals, and customs and by its use of language.[210]

The existence of an organized social life is by no means synonymous with the existence of a true community.[211] There is a clear distinction between common forms of cooperation and the nature of the true community. Common forms of cooperation focus merely on the accomplishment of an immediate need. The true community, by contrast, is forged by the identification of each individual self with the memory and hope of the community of which they are a part.[212] A typical mistake has frequently occurred when social groups have been given equivalent status with true communities.[213] Ultimately, the true community is distinguished by the ability its members demonstrate to build a common life

---

[207] Ibid., p. 388.

[208] Royce, J. The Problem of Christianity, vol. I, p. 166.

[209] Oppenheimer, Frank. op.cit., p. 343, 360. Several writers have suggested that Royce's early experiences in California during the Gold Rush left an indelible mark on his understanding of community. His book on California, for example, is considered to be a book outlining the basic framework of a social ethic which he subsequently developed in his later works.

[210] Royce, J. The Problem of Christianity, vol. I, p. 63.

[211] Royce, J. The Problem of Christianity, vol. II, p. 84.

[212] Ibid., p. 85.

[213] Ibid., p. 87.

together and extend it beyond themselves.[214]

This common understanding and goal provides the context within which the community can fulfill its fundamental responsibility of interpretation.[215] Within one's understanding of the community as a context for interpretation, one discovers the reality that a community exists wherever one individual attempts to interpret the mind of another individual. This intentionality at interpretation and understanding reflects the triadic process of interpretation.[216]

_____Within the community of interpretation, the individual who desires understanding pursues a five-fold process of interpretation. First, one regards another as a self. Then, one's past history and the history of the civilization of which one is a part, combines to establish the context for the interpretive process. Since the desire for interpretation arises from personal misunderstandings of one another, the process of interpretation fundamentally expresses the desire one's self has to be united with another self. Finally, simply understanding and interpreting another self is not enough. One must aim at something greater if the motivation for interpretation is to lead to a meaningful outcome.[217]

The desire to bridge the gap of disharmony through the unity of interpretation lies at the heart of Royce's argument for the central and primary role of the community. Clearly, every community fulfills a myriad of roles and responsibilities, but Royce's focus is to exhaust the primary ramifications implicit in the community as the horizon of meaning for interpretation.[218] In this role, the community establishes shared meanings, common traditions and an enduring heritage. In the context of community, moreover, religious self-consciousness is allowed to develop as it interprets its individual experiences in conversation with the shared meanings of the community.

Tradition, according to Royce, is critical in shaping an understanding of the role played by the key figures and texts in a particular religious community. It is tradition, and not historical experience, for example, which is responsible for

---

[214] Ibid., p. 88.
[215] Oppenheimer, Frank. op. cit., p. 353.
[216] Ibid., p. 354.
[217] Ibid., p. 355.
[218] Ibid., p. 358.

the view we have of Christ. Through tradition we read specific accounts of the master which in turn shape the interpretations we make regarding his life.[219] Apart from tradition we would have no view of Jesus.[220]

Even secondary Scriptures (i.e. Pauline writings) which reflect on the life of Jesus do so through the lens of interpretations shaped by tradition. Although William James denigrated the role of doctrine and tradition, Royce recognized correctly that doctrines and traditions were formed from the interpretations of our common social religious experience.[221]

Tradition also plays an important role in establishing the coherence of the religious community. Royce writes,

> But the community which he loves is rendered relatively constant in its will by its customs; yet these customs no longer seem, to the loyal individual, mere conventions or commands.[222]

Through traditions, customs and rules, an individual learns the spirit of interpretation which breeds loyalty to the community.[223]

By becoming aware of these traditions, customs and rules we become aware of the social will. Through the social will, moreover, we become more conscious of ourselves and the degree to which we willingly align ourselves in loyalty to the social will.[224] The social will creates coherence of focus in the individual and animates the spirit of the community by drawing loyal individuals into contact with the spirit underlying the customs and traditions of social cooperation.

Social cooperation, moreover, establishes languages and religions.[225] Thus, traditions, which result from social cooperation, give rise to language development and religious expression which, in turn, reflect the spirit of social

---

[219] Ibid., pp. 27-28.
[220] Ibid., p. 31.
[221] Royce, J. The Problem of Christianity, vol. I, p. xix.
[222] Ibid., p. 70.
[223] Ibid., p. 133.
[224] Ibid., p. 134.
[225] Royce, J. The Problem of Christianity, vol. II, p. 26.

cooperation that extends the meaning and significance of traditions.

Traditions, finally, provide unity and expression for the common social nature of our salvation. In the case of Christianity, for example, Paul's stress on the Lord's Supper established a common memory of our salvation. Through this tradition, the unity of communal life is cultivated and maintained.[226] Traditions keep the communal life of Christianity alive. By distilling the spirit of the Christian doctrine of life in traditions, these traditions preserve and transmit the essential spirit of Christianity: spiritual unity born of all who are loyal to the Beloved Community.[227]

The Sources of Religious Insight

These descriptions of the role traditions and doctrines play in shaping human consciousness through the role of the community placed Royce in direct conflict with his more famous friend and colleague, William James. Earlier, in The Varieties of Religious Experience, James had argued that the social experience of the church is secondary and superficial. Here, Royce illustrates how religious consciousness develops in religious community like an ascending spiral. The first level of individual experience gives rise to each successive new level. Each level continues upward until one can find the best overarching ideal which can unite all of these individual insights in a unified whole that provides meaning. Insight, moreover, is defined by Royce as that which provides the best explanation for the experience which one has had.

James had argued that the social experience of the church is secondary and superficial. By contrast, Royce exalted the role of the community in providing the one context within which experiences of the ambiguous, pluralistic universe could make sense.[228]

Royce's most sustained and deliberate disagreement with James is carried out in his popular work of 1912, Sources of Religious Insight. Royce begins with

---

[226] Ibid., p. 72.
[227] Ibid., p. 387.
[228] Royce, J. The Problem of Christianity, vol. I, p. XVI.

James' insight of individual religious experience. James had defined religious experience as the experience of individuals who regard themselves alone with the divine. But experience, on its own, is not sufficient to produce insight. Insight indicates a breadth of range, a unified view and a close personal touch. What individual religious experience teaches is our personal ideal and our personal need for salvation.[229]

The second source of religious insight is our social experience. Royce states that in our social experience we experience our need for salvation. Royce also states that we can have this experience without belonging to any specific form of religious faith. Although this appears to be a puzzling statement from one advocating our salvation as social, this insight will not gain salvific meaning until elevated to a new synthesis through the spirit of loyalty. Different religions develop differently because of the way in which different religious communities respond differently to religious needs. The role of the religious community in the interpretation of religious experience is illustrated by Royce when he writes,

> But in any case the plain man must needs interpret his vision of the ideal in terms consistent with his conception of God, or of the triumphant life, or of spiritual power, or in terms his traditions and his stage of personal development may suggest to him.[230]

Royce goes on to state that salvation comes by fostering brotherhood [sic] between all people. The human race can only be saved together, not separately.

The third source of religious insight is reason as the power to see widely and steadily and connectedly. Reason helps to draw a synthesis from the multiplicity of particular experiences. By the formation of a synthesis from this multiplicity an insight is won and this constitutes a legitimate religious experience.

This insight goes beyond the narrow limits James places on the right use

---

[229] Royce, J. Sources of Religious Insight. Originally published at Lake Forest, ILL: Lake Forest College, 1912; reprinted, 1977, pp. 1-34.
[230] Ibid., p. 52.

of reason. Reason, according to Royce, is not opposed to intuition, but acts to form broader intuitions. Therefore, its true enemy is not intuition, but a parochial outlook. Abstract reason cannot give us religious insight. Reason is a coherence-building faculty. Abstract reason does, however, provide us with the conceptions we need in order to prepare for intuitions and experiences that lie on higher levels.

At this level, reason creates a corporate consciousness which provides guidance for all opinions. This idea of corporate consciousness determines what the group will accept as true or false. This is corporate guidance in which true and false opinions are determined by the larger view to which the community of interpretation appeals. This corporate consciousness is anchored to the religious community and illustrates the way in which Royce sees the religious community acting to establish the framework for interpreting religious experience.

This definition is revolutionary. What Royce is stating is that all ideas of truth and error depend on the communal context. There is no universal moral ought. The community of interpretation provides the context in which one can evaluate the meaning of their conceptions of right and wrong, truth and error.[231]

The fourth source of insight is the role of the will in relationship to reason. Since reason guides the will to see a particular course of action, will must act to embrace this particular course in the satisfaction of the human need for salvation.[232]

All four of these sources of insight remain individual sources of insight unless elevated by the spirit of loyalty. Loyalty unifies as it elevates to a new level these four independent areas of awareness and experience: the *individual* need of salvation, the recognition that salvation is *social* through unity with all humanity, that *reason* can provide a reasonable and coherent view of truth and the *will* can take this insight and help the individual conform to this insight in order to fashion a plausible response to the human need to be saved.

Through loyalty, one establishes the social bonds which save. It is at the stage of loyalty that felt unities are first experienced. Through loyal deeds one apprehends the spirit of loyalty which leads one forward to self-actualization.

---

[231] Ibid., pp. 79-115.
[232] Ibid., pp. 119-161.

Royce defines the true principle of loyalty as,

> ...be loyal; so be loyal, that is, so seek, so accept, so
> serve your cause that thereby the loyalty of all your
> brethren till the world, through your example...
> through your own love of loyalty...will be furthered
> by your life.

By being loyal, an individual is able to create the coherence for understanding the religious nature of reality. Loyalty is the complete and practical devotion of a self to a cause.[233]

In constructing his religion of loyalty, Royce extends the role of loyalty by noting that the spirit of loyalty can redeem the pernicious reality of evil and suffering by placing it within a context which provides meaning. Suffering and evil take on a positive nature when they are given meaning. It is to experience the reality of suffering as a part of life and to recognize that suffering must be given meaning lest it destroy us.

Royce's insight on suffering is particularly instructive. Here, we are led to understand that what is so often seen as a barrier to religious belief can actually serve as a passageway. Suffering, as a part of human nature, can lead one into contact with the overarching ideal which gives all contingent particulars their meaning. Thus, Loyalty can redeem evil by developing within the individual a capacity to endure and to see the ultimate outcome of all evil in the universal Beloved Community of all who are loyal.[234]

This seventh source of insight, the unity of the spirit in the community of loyalty, culminates Royce's most spirited and sustained opposition to James' individualism. The unity of the spirit in the Beloved Community of loyalty is Royce's description of the way in which humans come in contact with the spirit which saves. By being loyal and exhibiting consistent loyalty, one is able to connect with the spirit of loyalty which saves by answering the human need for salvation through the community.

Loyalty is gained by joining with other loyal individuals who are

---

[233] Ibid., pp. 165-210.
[234] Ibid., pp. 213-254.

committed, in loyalty, to genuine causes. Common expressions of loyalty create a unity which captures the spirit of the Beloved Community of all who are loyal. Such finite expressions of loyalty create religious communities. These communities exhibit a variety of social forms which reflect the diversity of human persons who express loyalty in ways commensurate with the dynamics of their historical existence. Whether or not these finite communities are called religious communities will depend entirely on the way in which the members of the community define the nature and essence of their community.

Finite expressions of loyalty result in the formation of historic communities called the visible church. The visible church, according to Royce is an organization with a definite set of traditions, creeds, an accepted history, and a doctrine of divine revelation which constitute its origin and authority. The visible church exists to provide the context within which one can encounter their need for salvation and the satisfaction of this religious need.

It is within the visible church that all members of the invisible church, all who have been loyal, have found the context within which they have come into contact with the spirit of loyalty which saves. The invisible church is the spiritual brotherhood of all who have been loyal. It is not a human institution, but is built upon the visible institution and extends beyond it to spiritual union with all who are loyal. This is the ultimate expression and mediates the experience of salvation.

Royce amplified his position by emphasizing that the common core of religious experience was not the four qualities identified by James, but the religion of loyalty anchored in the religious community which alone provides salvation. Since the community, by definition, behaves as though it were autonomous, it asks its individual members to exhibit a love and devotion which no single individual, on its own, can sustain. This loving devotion of a self to a community takes precedence over self-love and is best defined as an expression of loyalty.[235]

Loyalty, moreover, is defined throughout as the willing and thoroughgoing

---

[235] Ibid., p. 68.

devotion of a self to a cause.[236]   Thus, love and loyalty really function as synonymous terms describing the same reality. Christian love, for example, is best exemplified by the spirit of loyalty.[237]   As such, love and loyalty in the context of community come to signify an individual's inability to realize these ideal values apart from the common life. Since it is the community within which these values are encountered, it is within this context that one encounters the Christ spirit which alone draws all towards their salvation by union with the community.[238]

Social Nature of Reality Realized in Communities

The significance of the individual being saved through the community is tied, once again, to the inherent social nature of reality.[239] Since we are essentially social animals, all of our development as individuals simply works to amplify the reality of sin, the need for grace, and our inability to find sin-satisfying grace on our own without the community.

Communities are both good and evil, depending on the spirit which they embody. Communities which foreshadow loyalty to the 'Beloved Community' inevitably become good. Communities which focus only on their limited ideals without working to transcend their own limitations in pursuit of loyalty to the 'Beloved Community' inevitably end in evil.[240]

In developing his idea of community, Royce is careful to distinguish between natural communities and communities of loyalty. Natural communities are ultimately communities of sin. The only escape from natural communities is through loyalty to a cause greater than the cause typified by one's natural community. Natural communities remain as such because they are unable to carry

---

[236] Ibid., pp. 68-69.
[237] Ibid., p. 98.
[238] Ibid., p. 99.
[239] Ibid., p. 149.
[240] Ibid., p. 168. Royce's treatment of good and evil communities foreshadows Tillich's treatment of the contrast between a finite and an ultimate concern. Finite concern inevitably is self- limiting. Ultimate concern, by contrast, leads one through all finite manifestations of finite concern to ultimate concern with the ground of being.

a person to a broader ideal. A natural community is formed from the accidents of nature and place. For example, to call oneself a Californian is to recognize one's identity only by one's natural citizenship.

Communities of loyalty, by contrast, save the individual by developing a loving devotion of a self to a cause. Here, a spiritual force draws one into defined communities. For example, to define yourself with a particular cause through a particular group through individual choice, is to recognize a larger reality than one experiences in natural communities. The difference between a natural community and a community of loyalty is that a community of loyalty has within itself the ability to transcend itself out of ultimate loyalty to the 'Beloved Community.'[241] There is a spiritual dimension which elevates. The creation of this community and the training of the individual to love this community cannot be devised by human initiative nor accomplished by human ingenuity alone.[242] This would be only a forced, transitory work. Instead, if in the midst of training in loyalty, one is able to catch a glimpse of the universal spirit of loyalty which transcends all finite communities, then one can be saved. This is why Paul argues that it is through the community of loyalty that one is saved.

The articulation by Paul of the community of loyalty captures the spirit of unity one realizes in common with all who are loyal.[243] Paul's initiative in developing loyalty to a cause commences the formation of a legitimate community. The formation of a legitimate community, captures the essence of the spirit of loyalty which, in turn, commences movement towards realization of the 'Beloved Community.'

The 'Beloved Community,' moreover, is synonymous with the symbol of the Kingdom of Heaven. It is the Beloved Community, as the Kingdom of Heaven, which, in its operations, transmits the spirit of loyalty which renders every human life significant and every human deed meaningful. In identifying and communicating its spiritual essence, the Beloved Community reflects its social nature in which the endless time-process captures the spirit of loyalty manifested

---

[241] Ibid., p. 179.
[242] Ibid., pp. 179-180.
[243] Ibid., p. 185.

throughout history.[244]

The only problem with Royce on this teaching is that he fails to recognize the various roadblocks that lie in the way of the realization of the Kingdom of Heaven.   Two, in particular, are quite prominent.   First, every religious community originally springs from a sectarian spirit.[245] It is only through growth and development that one softens specific perceptions in order to embrace a universal community of all believers.   Second, it is typical for every historical organization to become more preoccupied with its own life than with the life of God.[246]   Thus, as Royce maintains, it is imperative that the Christian doctrine of life always emphasize the significance of acting in line with the spirit of loyalty in order to hasten the coming of the 'Beloved Community.'[247]

The significance of Christianity's emphasis on the 'Beloved Community' is its supreme appeal to the fundamental social make-up of our nature. Christianity is the first religion, according to Royce, to make loyalty to the community not only impressive, but also transformative. This is the spirit which saves.   The human needs the community because without the community an individual is unable to remain loyal. The reason for this is that the community is itself a sign which must be interpreted.   As a result, it is both the context of interpretation and the mediating link between the individual human who needs to put their contingent experiences into a meaningful whole and the realm in which the overarching, coherence-producing ideal can be found.

The idea of sin is both personal and corporate. Personal sin is defined as those specific acts of betrayal against the community of which one is a part. Corporate sin, like Original Sin, is an effort to interpret why everyone is disloyal and needs the atoning spirit of the Beloved Community.[248] The idea or conception of Original Sin is a recognition of the universal reality of human evil. Therefore, rather than ignoring the reality of evil or pretending it does not exist, Royce wants to show how evil itself is a sign which in being interpreted, can lead to a reality

---

[244] Ibid., p. 355.
[245] Ibid., p. 358.
[246] Ibid., p. 359.
[247] Ibid., p. 360.
[248] Ibid., pp. 361-363.

beyond the particular sin act or evil act itself. By becoming and remaining loyal
to the community, the spirit of loyalty which forms the community atones for
one's sin through the release of its redemptive energy on the individual.

Royce further argues that the social nature of the community reflects our
inherent social nature.[249]   It is within the community that we can see a refracted
image of the spiritual unity of life. As conscious as we are of our individual needs
and identity, our common need and experience of community reflect the way in
which multiple individual consciousnesses can merge into a common social
consciousness sustained by loyalty.[250]

When viewed from the vantage point of the community, the individual
realizes he or she is not simply an isolated entity cut-off from all other entities.
Instead, an individual becomes aware of the way in which the community acts on
and through his or her individual life as he or she enters into common communal
consciousness.[251]

The Role of Hope and Memory

The defining mark of the community is the willful allegiance its members
show to a common event. In order for a community to be formed and sustained it
is necessary for individuals to identify with both a common past and a future
ideal. When such an identification is undertaken, then a common community can
be formed.

For Royce, ongoing interpretation of this common event signifies a
primary role hope and memory play in the interpretive process.   Hope, in
particular, is the spiritual and driving force in human transcendence. It is a power
which catapults the human onto a new level of reality. It prompts the setting aside
of parochial and provincial understandings born of natural communities to pursue
the more inclusive, ultimate, unifying ideal of the genuine community. Hope,
finally, elevates human consciousness beyond the particular structures in which

---

[249] Ibid., p. 421.
[250] Royce, J. The Problem of Christianity, vol. II, p. 28.
[251] Ibid., p. 29.

daily existence is embedded to a realm in which one can unite with the ultimate, unifying ideal of the Beloved Community of universal loyalty.

The first condition of this formation is the power of the individual to idealize one's life within the broader perimeters of the past, present, and future of the community.[252] This means the individual must integrate his or her individual consciousness into the communal consciousness of the community by identifying one's individual fortunes and misfortunes with the fortunes and misfortunes of one's community.[253]

A second aspect of community formation is the relation one takes not only to events and deeds, but also to entities and objects. Communal consciousness is formed by the relationship one's community forms to political institutions, social organizations and economic opportunities.[254] The relation of one's community to these entities and objects will fundamentally shape the individual consciousness of each of its members.[255]

Thus, a community is formed by the common life of individuals forged by the relationship of one's community to these entities and objects of one's attention. This relationship must be worked out historically. The community must be part of the time-process which extends into both the future and the past in grounding the self in the context of community.[256]

A third aspect of community formation is the capability to communicate. Individual selves must be capable of social communication. A community must continually revise its methods of communication in order to bring more and more individuals into meaningful interaction with one another. Standards to preserve communication must be undertaken. Methods of communication must be modified and revised.

The Early Church, for example, exemplifies these qualities inherent in the

---

[252] Ibid., p. 60.

[253] The present work of the Jewish community to help every Jew identify with the Holocaust reflects a similar effort. In this respect, the Holocaust event is the tragedy not only of the individuals and families directly touched by its tragedy, but also of every Jew who must face the evil that once threatened the very existence of the entire community.

[254] In Communities of Discourse, Robert Wuthnow highlights the significant impact social, political and economic organizations exerted on the rise of the Reformation.

[255] Royce, J. The Problem of Christianity, vol. II, p. 64.

[256] Ibid., p. 66.

formation of every community. It has identified with past Jewish history and anticipates the future in the consummation in the Kingdom of Heaven. It forged a distinct relationship with the Jewish Synagogue, the Roman government, and the cultural and economic entities current at its time. The Early Church also devised a form of communication which allowed its members to understand the significance of its origin in relation to previous activities outlined in the Hebrew Scriptures.[257]

The overriding issue in this entire discussion is to what extent a single entity like the church can be formed from a multiplicity of individual members. Royce's overwhelming answer is that an individual, in order to understand him or herself as an individual, must identify with a community. When identifying with a community, an individual must undertake to relate to the history of that community. In pursuing this relationship, an absolute consciousness of unity develops which allows many distinct individuals to define themselves through this common cooperation with the community.[258]

Thus, through the formative influences of the community, one is able to identify one's salvation with others who have preceded them. Through this identification, one identifies not only with the past history of one's community, but one's present relationship with other members of the community and one's future fortune as the community extends through time.

Ultimately, Royce argues that the idea of individual salvation is incomplete. We become immortal only by being a part of a community. Any individual isolated from conscious identity with a community will not only suffer alienation now, they will remain without salvation in the future.

Finally, in articulating the nature, need and formation of the community, Royce identifies the similarities between the spirit of the community and the Orthodox conception of the nature of God. In articulating this position, Royce writes,

> ...If a social order,...actually wins and keeps the love
> of its members; so that--...they still--with all their

---

[257] Ibid., p. 72.
[258] Ibid., p. 79, 83.

> whole hearts and their minds and their souls and
> their strength,--desire,...that such cooperations
> should go on...[259]

Thus, the social order, or the community, can cultivate the kind of loyalty and allegiance similar to the love and loyalty Jesus is recorded to have reserved for God alone.[260]

The Metaphysical Foundation of Religious Experience

In defending this position, moreover, Royce argues that this is not only empirically verifiable, but also metaphysically true. As stated in his introduction to The Problem of Christianity, Royce attempts to show that the reason human religious experience is manifested in this way is due to the metaphysical foundation of reality.[261] One must show, moreover, that this metaphysical foundation is necessary if one is to understand adequately how the spirit of loyalty which unifies and sustains communities and provides salvation transcends all finite and limited embodiments.[262]

Because the universal community is the doctrine which expresses the being, nature and manifestation of God, the identification and articulation of this doctrine is central. The unifying force in the universal community is the Spirit, which, according to Royce, is synonymous with the Christian symbol of the Holy Spirit.[263] It is the Spirit, as the unifying force in the universe, which illuminates our understanding of the metaphysical nature of the universe as community.[264] As such, it provides the reflective inquirer with the possibility of understanding, through interpretation, the role of Christianity both from the perspective of its effectiveness throughout history and from the perspective of providing the best explanation for the spiritual reality one experiences when one comes in contact

---

[259] Ibid., p. 91.
[260] Matthew 22:37-39.
[261] Royce, J. The Problem of Christianity, vol. I, p. xxxv.
[262] Royce, J. The Problem of Christianity, vol. II, p. 6.
[263] Ibid., p. 13.
[264] Ibid., p. 103.

with its spirit.[265]

By defining the problem of Christianity in this way, Royce pursues an understanding of the nature of one's meaning as an individual by contextualizing the self in a social approach to metaphysics.[266] It is not only that one's conscious acts as an individual reflects a sub-conscious awareness of belonging to a group. Royce argues that the fundamental ground of reality is social and that the metaphysical ground of one's being as an individual is social.[267] Thus, the world is a community with a time-process.

In demonstrating the way in which the world is a community with a time-process Royce turns to natural science and the specific work of Charles Peirce to demonstrate that both the natural world and the mental life possess inbuilt dynamisms that give signs of preferring life to death and meaning and value to nihilism and chance.[268] Drawing specifically on the evolutionary process inherent in natural science, Royce expands this theory in order to demonstrate the way in which the entire universe of mind and matter is progressing towards the universal community of all who are loyal. Royce is not trying to prove the scientific reliability of the evolutionary process.

By contrast, Royce wants to demonstrate the way in which the idea of the evolutionary process best illuminates the way in which a grand unifying ideal can gather all finite particulars of mind and matter into a unified, meaningful whole which makes sense.[269] In a move reminiscent of Hegel's 'Geist,' Royce identifies the spiritual force of the evolutionary process with the divine spirit of interpretation, present throughout the universe, and guiding the universe in all of its processes towards a more genuine community of all who are loyal. It is in this way that Royce establishes the validity of the world as a community with a time-process in which all finite particulars of mind and matter can be interpreted in a progressive manner in order to realize the ideal of the universal Beloved

---

[265] Ibid., p. 104.
[266] Oppenheimer, Frank. op. cit., p. 345.
[267] Ibid., p. 350.
[268] Oppenheim, Frank. Royce's Mature Philosophy of Religion. Notre Dame, IN: University of Notre Dame Press, 1987, p. 165.
[269] Royce, J. The Problem of Christianity, vol. II, pp. 420-430.

Community of all who are loyal.

According to Royce, the real world is, in its wholeness, a community.[270] Therefore, the fundamental nature of reality is community. The world has the structure of a community.[271] Through the time-process, the real world strives to achieve the Universal Community as a demonstration of its fundamental spirit and expression of reality. Thus, within the whole time-process, the world is imbued with signs which must be interpreted.

We are not isolated individuals with impenetrable relations to one another. We are fundamentally social individuals whose membrane of consciousness is shaped and penetrated by our social relations. Our true nature causes us to gather into classes and societies as a manifestation of this genuine reality. Genuine reality, moreover, is an attempt to define what we experience when we claim to experience. As such, Royce defines genuine reality as that which can be experienced by a multiplicity of minds while unreality is defined as that which is experienced alone.[272] Royce suggests that both individuals and communities are real with their own type of reality. Thus, when one makes a claim that an object is real, the individual is stating that one's personal experience of this reality coincides with how the community has determined or defined the way in which an individual will experience an object as real.

The Individual and the Collective

In defining his metaphysical theory in this way, Royce amplifies his thesis by suggesting that every tension within historical contingencies lays in understanding the relationship of the individual to the community. Thus, once again, the historical and the metaphysical fundamentally reflect one another.[273] In the specific case of American life, Royce identifies the persistent and corrosive tendencies towards one of two extremes: a radical individualism with no regard

---

[270] Royce, J. The Problem of Christianity, vol. II, p. 279.
[271] Ibid., p. 375.
[272] Oppenheimer, Frank. op. cit., p. 351.
[273] Linnell E. Cady, "A Model for a Public Theology," Harvard Theological Review, 80:193-212, April, 1987, pp. 204-05.

for the community or an incipient collectivism in which all individualism is destroyed.[274] This pernicious and persistent antagonism can be overcome only by the willing, voluntary devotion of the individual to a community.

The individual, by him or herself, is unable to find meaning for his or her life. The individual develops meaning only as he or she enters into community with other selves.[275] In community with other selves, one evolves to a level of consciousness uninhabitable on one's own, in which the spiritual ideal which can unify life is realized. On this higher level, the consciousness of the individual is fundamentally shaped by the consciousness of the community to which the individual has voluntarily submitted through loyalty. Thus, an internal meaning of an individual is shaped by its external expression with other members of the community.

In extending Royce's theory of the origin and destiny of the self, Royce declares in the Philosophy of Loyalty that,

> ...a man's self has no contents, no plans, no purposes, except those which are, in one way or another, defined for him by his social relations.[276]

Sounding a bit fatalistic, Royce nevertheless extends his line of reasoning by suggesting that imitation of social relations is necessary because social relations mediate the forms of self-expression which have meaning in one's communal context.[277] Thus, it is within a communal context that one learns how to interpret the multiplicity of stimuli from the external environment. It is also within a communal context that one learns the various beliefs and actions which mediate this understanding of the external world.

To a limited extent, Royce suggests that it is by the loyal devotion to a community that one is able to transcend one's self. This act of self-transcendence

---

[274] Ibid., p. 205.
[275] Oppenheimer, Frank. op. cit., p. 342.
[276] Royce, Josiah. The Philosophy of Loyalty. Originally published in 1908 by MacMillan and Co. Published in 1983 by University of Chicago Press, Chicago, IL., p. 94.
[277] Ignas Skrupskelis argues this point in his discussion of Royce's philosophy of loyalty. See Ignas K Skrupskelis, "Royce and the Justification of Authority," Southern Journal of Philosophy, 8, pp. 165-170, Summer-Fall, 1970, p. 167.

leads one into a recognition of something other than one's self. In such a case, one recognizes one's individual limitations and awakens to one's individual need and longing for spiritual unity in community. Unless such an awakening occurs, however, the religious answer to this human dilemma will remain unnoticed.[278]

In distinguishing between various sources of religious insight, Royce is careful to emphasize that individual need can only be reconciled in a communal context. Since it is within the community that the individual is saved, then the community, in whatever form, holds the potential as the sign which, if interpreted properly, can lead to the universal source of salvation.

Royce offers an important emphasis here which is worth noting. Because salvation is social, and because reality is social, the essential nature of reality is to produce universal salvation.[279] This universal interpretation places Royce's discussion at odds not only with those who say there is a different universal explanation, but also with those who say not all religions are primarily concerned with salvation. Nevertheless, if experience has shown an individual his or her need of salvation, then the religious problems addressed by Christianity are already upon him or her.[280]

But how do we account for the variety and disharmony so apparent among the world's religions? Royce begins by noting that the religious consciousness of humanity is going to appear in many different forms with conflicting notions. This fact, however, does not dispel the unity of the religious concerns of humanity.[281] Eventually, all humans who awaken to their spiritual need, recognize the necessity of encountering the solution to this need in a social context. The social context is not going to solve all needs an individual defines as religious, but it will meet the primary ones.[282]

The religious community is the context in which the human eventually discovers the spiritual reality of the unity of one's life that places so many fluctuating desires into harmony as a meaningful whole. The community unifies

---

[278] Royce, Josiah. Sources of Religious Insight, p. 32.
[279] Ibid., p. 37.
[280] Ibid., p. 38.
[281] Ibid., p. 42.
[282] Ibid., p. 44.

desires and provides a synthesizing guide to one's purpose in life. Ultimately, the unity-of-life one experiences in community awakens one to the ideal of life which is synonymous with God's will.[283]

The formation of an ideal reflects an interpretation of whatever conception of God, of life, or of spiritual power one's traditions and personal development has suggested. This is a primary reason why so many different religions emerge as they provide a variety of interpretations to life as people know and experience it.[284] Periodically, one catches a glimpse of this ideal life. But, alone, one cannot sustain this glimpse. As a result, individuals are drawn into a communal context which exists to sustain this ideal.

Throughout his work Royce repeatedly spars with William James. In discussing the nature and role of the religious community, he is no different. According to Royce, the problem of salvation for William James is primarily individual. Religious experience, in its pure form, is an experience of an individual alone with the divine. All social aspects of religion, according to James, are corruptions of the pure form of individual religious experience.[285] Ultimately, James believes that pure religion cannot be found in any form of social experience.[286] The point Royce believes James has missed lies at the very heart of their disagreement. James is wedded to an Enlightenment conception of the self in which all meaning is constituted by the self before the community. Royce, by contrast, does not believe the human, on his or her own, can sustain meaning for him or herself. Therefore, individual experiences, for Royce, must be the material from which interpretation forms bridges or bonds to a spiritual realm in which these experiences make sense.

Beyond his emphasis on religion as social, Royce also sees religion as cumulative and developmental.[287] The development of religious consciousness develops over time as an internal dialogue between the self and the not-self. This

---

[283] Ibid., p. 43.
[284] Ibid., p. 53.
[285] Ibid., p. 62.
[286] Ibid., p. 63.
[287] Royce, Josiah. The Problem of Christianity, vol., pp. 18-19.

dialogue broadens to include the individual self and the social self.[288]   Modes of communication, cultural beliefs, traditions, and modes of behavior sanctioned or censored by the community all are signs which contribute to the development of religious consciousness.   These signs   stimulate the activity of interpretation which takes one from one's contingent reality into the spiritual realm wherein the unity of life is found.[289]

As this consciousness develops one becomes aware of the way in which higher forms of the communal life split with lower forms of the communal life.[290] The development of this consciousness is intensified as one becomes aware of one's individual relation to the collective.[291]   The 'Beloved Community,' as the ultimate ground of reality, both embodies and stimulates the values and ideals which no human individual, viewed as an unencumbered self, could remotely approach.[292]

Royce expands his treatment of the individual and the community by suggesting that this distinction led to the articulation by the Christian Church of the doctrine of the Trinity. The doctrine of the Trinity is an attempt to explain how the individual doctrine of God as transcendent, Jesus as the master who taught the mystery of the Kingdom, and the emergence of the Church are all held together in a common community.[293] This doctrine, more than any other, expresses the relation of individual entities to the common collective. It is the awareness of these two levels, moreover, which leads one to an awareness of the Christian doctrine of life. Within this common doctrine of life is the recognition that people are not only individuals separated by distinct consciousness, but also members with one another in a universal community.[294]

---

[288] Valsiner and Van der Veer discuss the significance of this emphasis in Royce. See J. Valsiner and R. Van DerVeer, "On the Social Nature of Human Cognition: An Analysis of the Shared Intellectual Roots of George Herbert Mead and Lev Vygotsky," Journal for the Theory of Social Behaviour, 1988, 18, 1, March, pp. 117-136; p. 123.

[289] John E. Smith makes this point in a comparative analysis he makes between Royce and Dewey. See, John E. Smith, "The Value of Community: Dewey and Royce," Southern Journal of Philosophy, 12, pp. 469-479, Winter, 1974; p. 469.

[290] Ibid., p. 478.

[291] Royce, J. The Problem of Christianity, vol. I, p. 152.

[292] Ibid., p. 173.

[293] Ibid., p. 204.

[294] Royce, J. The Problem of Christianity, vol. II, p. 24.

The Nature of Communities

Because the Gospel of John expresses the need for the transformation of the individual through the community, it is the preferred Gospel.[295] The transformation which the individual seeks is mediated by a united community expressing love. This understanding, moreover, is reflected by Paul and his interpretation that the church is synonymous with the presence of the Lord.[296] Thus, Christ is spiritually present whenever the loyal, faithful members of the universal community gather.

In identifying Christ's presence with the presence of the church, Royce further argues that one's salvation is tied to one's relationship to this community. Clearly, there are a variety of forms of religious community, but the Christian Church, in its articulation of salvation through loyalty to the community, is the most significant. Yet, does the visible form of the Christian Church reflect the community of loyalty which Royce claims is necessary? Certainly not, but it is a sign of the higher community.

In its purest form the true church remains an invisible church.[297] Various manifestations of religious communities exist, but none can fulfill the ultimate purpose of the true church nor dispel the reliance individuals must display in seeking their salvation through the church.[298] Without a doubt, organized religion is in decline. But this decline has not removed the human problem of finding meaning and salvation for life through the religious community. As a result, every age must provide signs that can be interpreted for those who seek to find satisfaction for their needs through religious community.

But the true church, as an interpreted sign of the visible church, captures the universal spirit of loyalty present in the organized social life devoted to unifying all humankind in one common spirit.[299] Because individual human

---

[295] Royce, J. The Problem of Christianity, vol. I, p. 207.
[296] Ibid., p. 107.
[297] Ibid., p. 115.
[298] Ibid., p. 232.
[299] Royce, J. The Problem of Christianity, vol. II, p. 367.

consciousness is limited, the need for a wider social outlook is paramount.[300] By gaining a wider social outlook, we join a larger unity of consciousness. These larger unities of consciousness, moreover, express the various forms of the spirit and shape consciousness through their manifestations of the spirit of loyalty.[301] Basically, Royce suggests that the invisible church consists of those who have recognized the true spirit of salvation mediated through displays of loyalty to particular organizations devoted to honorable causes.[302].

In an effort to identify legitimate sources of community-forming loyalty, Royce provides a checklist which establishes criteria for evaluating the nature of loyalty. Is it a fitting cause of loyalty? Does it so serve its cause that one can move beyond specific objects of loyalty to unity with the divine spirit of loyalty? Does the influence of its loyalty extend to the establishment of the 'Beloved Community.' All three questions reflect Royce's conviction that training in particular forms of loyalty can lead one to an insight which both unifies and transcends all other sources of religious insight by providing a unifying ideal.[303]

Loyalty allows one to pursue the divine will. The divine will draws all humanity into a common unity.[304] Since loyalty can only be displayed in community, it is essential that one gather in community in order to pursue fulfillment of the divine will. It is also important to gather into community in order that through the community one can seek salvation by finding the spirit of loyalty as the mark of the invisible, true church.[305] All members of the invisible church belong to religious communities, but all members of religious communities do not necessarily belong to the invisible church.[306] As a result, the spirit of loyalty, as the centerpiece of the invisible church, is experienced and defined by its embodiment of religious consciousness in community.

In identifying loyalty as the centerpiece of religious consciousness the religious nature of communities is now identified. Communities exist as both

---

[300] Royce, J. Source of Religious Insight, p. 263.
[301] Ibid., p. 273.
[302] Ibid., p. 275.
[303] Ibid., p. 276.
[304] Ibid., pp. 276-277.
[305] Ibid., p. 280.
[306] Ibid., p. 281.

contexts of interpretation and signs which can be interpreted. Because finite communities allow one to connect with the infinite Beloved Community, they are fundamental to the interpretive process.

The Religious Nature of the True Community

Loyalty is the centerpiece of Royce's religious philosophy. The spirit of loyalty provides the foundation for a community within which one can find a philosophy of life, a religion which is plausible, and an explanatory principle of the universal need and nature of salvation.[307]   Loyalty, moreover, is, "...the willing and practical and thoroughgoing devotion of a person to a cause."[308]   To capture the essence of loyalty, an individual must have a cause to which one is loyal, be thoroughly devoted to it, and be able to express one's devotion in a sustained and practical way. Elsewhere, Royce emphasizes that loyalty is the practically devoted love of an individual for a community.[309]   Through this devotion, one comes in contact with the spirit which saves.

The guiding force of loyalty is outlined by Royce in the following way,

> So serve your cause...that through your service everybody whom you influence will be a more devoted servant of his own cause, and thereby of the cause of causes--the unity of all the loyal.[310]

This expression of loyalty in service to one's cause captures the heart of the religion of loyalty. According to Royce, loyalty is the religion which satisfies, at once, four of the central needs of a human: an individual need for salvation, a social need to be united with others, a rational need for a coherent view of truth, and a need to align our life with the master principle of life willingly.[311]

Loyalty is the synthesizing activity which unites all four individual needs

---

[307] Royce, J. The Problem of Christianity, vol. I, p. VII.
[308] Royce, J. The Philosophy of Loyalty, p. 861.
[309] Royce, J. The Problem of Christianity, vol. I, p. xvii, 169.
[310] Royce, J. Sources of Religious Insight, p. 292.
[311] Ibid., p. 166.

into a coherent whole. The practice of loyalty creates the context within which our individual needs can be met. Loyalty both defines the highest goal of life and the difficulty one faces in attaining it.[312] As a religious expression, loyalty recognizes the universal human need for salvation and the universal inability to achieve salvation on one's own.

The principle and practice of loyalty not only forms the heart of Royce's religious philosophy, but also that of his ethics. Through the exercise of loyalty one gains direction for one's life.[313] Loyalty inclines an individual self to complete itself through unity and devotion to a social self. Without this deliberate devotion to a social self, an individual self remains meaningless and lost: alone and without salvation.[314]

As a result of the human need for salvation and the human inability to achieve salvation, one often confuses one's religious need with one's moral obligation. Clearly, moral questions accompany religious concerns. But the two are not synonymous. Moral questions serve one's religious concerns with salvation when they highlight one's moral failures which, in turn, can be interpreted. In this way, the inability to live up to one's moral ideals can serve as a sign which awakens one to the need for grace.[315]

Royce's moral imperative illustrates how moral failure can awaken one to his or her need for grace. Royce writes, "...so act as never to have reason to regret the principle of your action."[316] This, of course, is impossible. It is impossible to act with such breadth of perspective that one never regrets an earlier deed. Even if one lives every day with loyalty and devotion to a chosen cause only a person with an arrested development could look back on earlier expressions of loyalty without some measure of regret. Thus, grace becomes the spiritual experience of communal forgiveness for one's regretted past actions. In this way, moral failure awakens an individual to his or her religious need by establishing a sign that can be interpreted. By being interpreted, the moral failure can lead an individual to

---

[312] Ibid., p. 171.
[313] Royce, J. The Problem of Christianity, vol. II, p. 98.
[314] Oppenheimer, Frank. op. cit., p. 343.
[315] Royce, J. Sources of Religious Insight, p. 181.
[316] Ibid., p. 189.

salvation through his or her expression of loyalty to a religious community.[317]

The need for grace becomes even more obvious when one is disloyal. Since the greatest expression of loyalty is the pursuit of spiritual unity, the greatest expression of disloyalty is the performance of deeds which dissolve this spiritual unity. Because loyalty is the practical devotion to a cause, and because disloyalty is the practical betrayal of a cause, grace is the activity of the community in restoring a disloyal member back to citizenship in the cause in order that he or she may again become an expression of the spirit of loyalty.

The Role of the Will

Critical to the exercise of loyalty is the orientation of the will. In defining the will, Royce acknowledged his indebtedness to Schopenhauer with an appropriate change. Royce suggests that there are three basic attitudes of the will: the will to live, the denial of the will to live, and the will to be loyal.[318] In exercising the will to be loyal, one expresses the activity of the will which unites the individual self with the social self.

By implication, loyalty draws one into relationship with a cause greater than oneself.[319] But the individual always runs the risk of aligning one's individual will with a cause which neither sustains nor serves the universal cause of loyalty. This reflects Royce's concern with having an ultimate destiny which one might miss. Thus, how does one determine the legitimate from the illegitimate causes to which one should be loyal?

Royce claims there are at least three causes or expressions of causes which deserve humanity's loyalty and function as expressions of will: "Patriotism," exemplified by the willingness to die for one's country, "martyrdom," exemplified by the willingness to die for one's faith, and "duty," exemplified by the orientation of one's will.[320] Patriotism and martyrdom both teach that certain causes deserve the loyalty of its citizens or followers because they elevate the

---

[317] loc. cit.
[318] Royce, J. The Problem of Christianity, vol. II, p. 298; 305; 309.
[319] Royce, J. The Philosophy of Loyalty, p. 860.
[320] Ibid., p. 861; 873.

individual life into contact with a spiritual ideal which provides meaning. Duty teaches the necessity of aligning one's will with the causes deserving loyalty. Together, patriotism, martyrdom and duty combine to illustrate the necessity of loyalty realized in and through the establishment and perpetuation of the community.[321]

Loyalty, moreover, is never simply an emotion. Loyalty, for its proper exercise, requires the restraint and submission of one's natural desires to a cause. Loyalty is the result of self-control. It is expressed through a variety of forms of service. It is learned by imitation, but moves beyond mere imitation as a form of self-expression.[322] As a form of self-expression, moreover, loyalty is duty expressed as a form of one's will coming to rational consciousness.[323]

Loyalty originates deliberately through the exercise of individual choice. But this exercise of choice is anchored to the emergence of an individual or a cause who can inspire the willing devotion of a self in loyalty. This expression of individual choice through loyalty to a cause initiates an interconnectedness between individuals who express loyalty to particular causes and the communities which emerge from these causes who are worthy of such expressions of love and loyalty.[324]

Royce returns to the example of Paul in order to amplify this point. Royce suggests that Christ's impact on Paul is a result of Paul's willing engagement, through interpretation, with the spirit of Christ. It is Paul's interpretation of Christ's person and work and not Christ himself who impacts Paul. This impact, moreover, leads to the establishment of the Pauline communities as the Early Church which become the centers of the spirit of love expressed as loyalty in which an individual can experience their salvation.[325]

Patriotism, martyrdom and duty, as expressions of loyalty, all lead one beyond self-love to social love. Social love is the expression of passion for causes beyond oneself which intensify self-consciousness and make one determined to

---

[321] Ibid., p. 865.
[322] Ibid., p. 868.
[323] Ibid., p. 869.
[324] Royce, J. The Problem of Christianity, vol. I, p. 185.
[325] Ibid., pp. 188-189.

serve a cause greater than oneself.[326]   Loyalty, as the source of this passion, helps fix one's attention upon some one cause, helps one unite with others in this cause, shows one the place of action in serving this cause, and says that in such service one's salvation will be found.

Loyalty, moreover, exists at all levels of society.[327]   It operates to unite the different spheres of life into a developmental whole. Loyalty is the attitude one exhibits which reflects one's love of God. Loyalty provides the orientation to society which, in turn, can provide the one overarching ideal we need to govern our life.[328]

Although loyalty to the community is often juxtaposed to individualism, it is not in opposition to individual identity.   Loyalty is not opposed to individualism.   Loyalty simply teaches that individualism, on its own, cannot produce a social cause or overarching ideal which unifies life. Individualism has provided necessary correctives for misplaced social causes.[329] Nevertheless, when individualism is exalted as the unifying ideal, commitment to the social ideals which ultimately save one is lost.

Royce returns to the question if loyalty is supreme what objects remain worthy of our loyalty? At its core, the object which is worthy of one's loyalty must be capable of joining many persons into the unity of a single life. There are several levels which identify objects worthy of one's loyalty including personal friendship, one's nuclear and extended family, and one's state and country. All of these relationships are sign-producing realities which not only reflect objects worthy of loyalty, but also place one in contact with the spirit that saves.[330]

In contrast to these objects of legitimate loyalty, however, various social groups demand loyalty which do not operate with interest in the common good. In some cases, what begins as a source of legitimate loyalty can, in fact, turn bad. Frequently, this is a result of two or more objects demanding loyalty to

---

[326] Royce, J. The Philosophy of Loyalty, p. 871.
[327] Ibid., p. 876.
[328] Ibid., pp. 876-877.
[329] Ibid., pp. 881-882.
[330] Ibid., p. 897.

themselves over the higher good of universal loyalty.[331]

Typically, this clash results from a violation of Royce's basic premise for evaluating legitimate objects of our loyalty. Royce emphasizes that loyalty results from the exercise of choice. The exercise of choice, moreover, should be inclined towards those objects which produce more loyalty in the world rather than less.[332] Ultimately, the greatest choice one can make is to exercise choice in such a way that loyalty is able to prosper among all people.[333]

True loyalty should be both the highest expression of one's private passion and the way in which one conforms in one's public life.[334] True loyalty should be so pure that it does not arouse the hatred in another nor injure anyone else's opportunity to be loyal. Ideally, true loyalty should evolve and grow. The process by which loyalty evolves and grows fulfills its nature as the manifestation of the universal law and spiritual essence of reality.[335]

The Universal and the Particular and the Development of a New Consciousness

Loyalty, by its very nature, is a universal ideal. It represents a supreme good and is universally accessible.[336] Because it is universally accessible it provides unity-of-life at every level in which it is exhibited.[337]

Through the exercise of loyalty one establishes one's conscience. Thus, one's conscience is relative to one's culture, but universal in its origin.[338] Loyalty establishes the universal moral law. Every individual is called to be loyal, to identify a special object of one's loyalty, to find oneself within the object of one's loyalty, and to transcend the particular cause to find the universal unity of all

---

[331] Ibid., p. 901.
[332] Ibid., p. 902.
[333] Ibid., p. 904.
[334] Ibid., p. 906.
[335] Ibid., p. 913.
[336] Ibid., p. 914.
[337] Ibid., p. 922.
[338] Ibid., p. 923.

people who express loyal devotion to a cause.[339]

In the particular context of America, the call for loyalty becomes acute. Through the active exercise of loyalty, one learns that loyalty is the central integrating principle of life. Concomitant with this discovery, however, is the recognition that loyalty must continually work in a social context which is ever-changing and expanding.[340] That is to say, the social, historical, and contingent context is full of signs which can convey contact with an ultimate ideal if interpreted properly.

Because loyalty is not sufficiently practiced it must be taught. The first context in which one can teach loyalty is through one's immediate family. Unfortunately, family ties are disintegrating. With this disintegration the initial and primary context for learning loyalty no longer exists.[341]

With the disintegration of the family other social groups have been substituted as sources for cultivating one's loyalty. Political organizations, athletic teams and trade unions are only a few of the many social organizations which elicit some level of loyal devotion.[342] But there is no guarantee that they operate either for good or for evil.

In fact, these different social organizations, which reflect various embodiments of finite social organizations, often exalt their finite concerns to ultimate, universal concerns. That is to say, they make the loyalty they demand of their constituents ultimate rather than contingent. They refuse to see their organization as a sign in the interpretive development of loyalty and, instead, insist that their organization is the final stage in the development of loyalty. The result is an insistence on loyalty to their cause with the disintegrating effect that one's need for an ultimate, overarching ideal cannot be found.[343]

Clearly, these organizations are useful for training individuals in loyalty. In fact, Royce is careful to emphasize that smaller segments of society are the best place to begin in one's development of an understanding of loyalty. Through

---

[339] Ibid., p. 934.
[340] Ibid., p. 939.
[341] Ibid., p. 942.
[342] Ibid., p. 946.
[343] Ibid., p. 947.

loyalty to one's state or province, for example, one can learn the spiritual essence of loyalty which later can be turned into loyalty to the nation.[344]

In order to sustain loyalty, moreover, the members of a community must have role models and ideals worthy of their allegiance.[345] In identifying with role models and promoting the pursuit of ideals, an individual, joined to the community through loyalty, is sustained in this allegiance by self-identification with these individuals and causes.

The role models and ideals represent an ultimate cause worthy of loyalty. This ultimate cause unites several individual lives into a common life.[346] As this unity occurs, moreover, it leads to the cultivation of the ultimate ideal in which the harmony of all causes is identified with one all-embracing cause.[347] The development of this ideal represents Royce's fundamental conviction that loyalty must develop through elemental forms to more sophisticated expressions.[348] Through this development, moreover, one is able to perceive the rational unity and goodness of the world, is capable of recognizing the fullness of meaning despite our limited personal experience of this meaning, and is able to express confidence in the ultimate nature and goal of the world.[349]

The exercise of loyalty ultimately develops a new self-consciousness.[350] Throughout Royce's later writings (The Philosophy of Loyalty, Sources of Religious Insight, and The Problem of Christianity) the exercise of loyalty is seen as an elevation of the human spirit. As the spiritual center of Royce's religious philosophy, loyalty creates a higher consciousness in the human.[351] By elevating human consciousness to a new level, loyalty, whether in its Christian form or in any other form, allows an individual to discern that one's greatest good is served

---

[344]Ibid., p. 953.

[345] Ibid., p. 962.

[346] Ibid., p. 994.

[347] Ibid., p. 1004.

[348] Ibid., p. 1007.

[349] Ibid., p. 1010.

[350] Royce, Josiah. The Letters of Josiah Royce. Edited with an introduction by John Clendenning. Chicago: The University of Chicago Press, 1970; p. 359. Royce borrows from Hegel's use of the correlation of growing self-consciousness and social surroundings to make this point.

[351] Royce, J. The Problem of Christianity, vol. I, p. 158.

by faithfulness to the community.[352]

Loyalty to the community is synonymous with the love of God.[353] Thus, loyalty to the community, as a primary expression of our love of God, is the source of our salvation.[354] Loyalty saves in that it not only teaches the individual the nature of reality, but also allows the individual to influence the lives of other individuals in the cause of universal loyalty.[355]

Charity and justice are the two primary fruits of the loyal spirit. Charity and justice are the foundation for achieving a universal community of loyalty.[356] The expression of charity and justice by loyal people draws people not yet members of the community into the community of loyalty.[357] Through identification with the community of loyalty, human consciousness is able to rise to identify with the universal community.

Loyalty is, in the final analysis, the expression of a practical faith that communities have a value which is superior to all the values and interests of detached individuals.[358] The expression of loyalty forms, in every individual that expresses it, a community out of formerly detached individuals. But loyalty cannot be confined to tribal solidarity, family ties, or national identities. The universal community of loyalty supersedes all of these finite particulars.[359] Loyalty is powerful enough to overcome our natural disposition to independence and individuality, but it needs these entities as part of the sign process out of which it can be interpreted.[360]

---

[352] Royce, J. The Problem of Christianity, vol. II, p. 99.
[353] Royce, J. The Problem of Christianity, vol. I, p. 408.
[354] Ibid., p. 410.
[355] Royce, J. Sources of Religious Insight, p. 202.
[356] Ibid., p. 205.
[357] Royce, J. The Problem of Christianity, vol. II, p. 101.
[358] Royce, J. The Problem of Christianity, vol. I, p. 72.
[359] Ibid., p. 170.
[360] Ibid., p. 182.

Love as Loyalty

Finally, Royce equates loyalty with love. Love, in Christian terms, is best expressed as loyalty. Love as loyalty is not simply an emotion, but an entire orientation and interpretation of life.[361] It is this love which completes the consciousness of the community as a community.

It is through love that individuals become anchored to the community. This anchor allows individual consciousness to be molded by the communal consciousness of the community. Love not only creates communal consciousness, but also works to preserve it.[362] Love, as loyalty, establishes the basis for the consciousness of the community which human reason alone cannot produce. Such love helps one recognize that it is through the spiritual unity of the loyal that insight is gained and salvation is won.[363]

Salvation through love as loyalty is necessary because as individuals we are not only lost, but also are entirely incapable of attaining our salvation on our own.[364] Salvation is necessary because as individuals we are often confused between our natural loves and our enlightened loves. Natural love results from the natural communities of which we are a part--families, communities, countries. Without enlightenment, however, natural loves cannot save us. In fact, they become the very enemy of the cultivation and realization of the universal community.

Enlightened love, or loyalty, takes time. It can be taught. It can develop. Enlightened love not only draws you into membership in the universal community, but also releases the power of the 'Beloved Community' to act upon you.[365] This love, unfortunately, is often misunderstood. Enlightened love is often taken to mean self-abnegation or pure altruism.[366] But this is simply not the case.

---

[361] Royce, J. The Problem of Christianity, vol. II, p. 98.
[362] Ibid., p. 92.
[363] Ibid., pp. 90-92.
[364] Royce, J. The Problem of Christianity, vol. I, p. 374.
[365] Ibid., p. 158.
[366] Ibid., p. 79.

Enlightened love is the same love Paul taught through his interpretation of the sayings and parables of Jesus.[367] Paul's interpretation created a new consciousness within the Early Church that shaped Jesus' teachings into a coherent whole capable of transforming the members of the Christian community. Enlightened love embodies the saving power of Jesus' teachings to love the Lord your God with your heart, soul, mind and strength and your neighbor as yourself.[368] As such, enlightened love teaches its adherents to embrace a positive attitude of love towards life and to work out the practical implications of this love through one's community.

Contemporary Discussions Concerning the Role of the Religious Community as Anticipated by Royce

Royce's discussion of the true nature of the community is a helpful corrective to an exclusive focus on 'religionless religion.' Royce's focus, moreover, has helped to recover the important role of the religious community. From general surveys of American culture to intellectual developments within specific disciplines, interest in the role and function of the religious community is not only growing, but is becoming primary.[369] Although some recent theological inquiry has noted the tendency of the American church to ignore or diminish the importance of the religious community,[370] virtually every major religious tradition is renewing its interest in the importance of the community in providing meaning and understanding for religious faith.

The quest for religious faith matters because it is here that one finds the unity in one's life that allows all discordant experiences to make sense. In each

---

[367] Ibid., p. 114.
[368] Ibid., p. 75.
[369] Several examples worth noting include: Gallup Poll, Religion in America, 1993; Bellah, Robert, et. al. Habits of the Heart, San Francisco: Harper and Row, Pub., 1985; Wuthnow, Robert. Rediscovering the Sacred: Perspectives on Religion in Contemporary Society, Princeton: Princeton University Press, 1988; several books edited by Stephen Katz which focus on religious experience and religious tradition. All of these books share the common theme of the primary role of the religious community in the religious quest.
[370] Jack Verheyden, "The Invisibility of the Church in American Protestant Theology and the Issue of Catholic Reality," Occasional Paper, School of Theology at Claremont, Claremont, CA., Vol. 4, #3, December, 1994.

religious context, moreover, a variety of paths of preparation are offered to assist the individual in this process. This quest is not pursued or accomplished apart from a communal context. It is interpreted to the individual through the traditions and history of one's religious community.

To illustrate, consider two examples from Western religious traditions, one from the Hebrew Scriptures, the other from the Christian Scriptures. In I Samuel 3, Eli and Samuel are in the private quarters of the Temple, almost asleep, when Samuel hears a voice he interprets as Eli's. Three times he hears the voice, believing each time that it is Eli's. From the text, it is apparent that Samuel has not yet acquired the categories to interpret the voice as originating in God. Subsequent to the third encounter, however, Eli interprets that the voice is coming from God, although there is no indication that he has ever heard the voice himself. Nevertheless, he gives Samuel specific instructions regarding how he should respond. Eventually, Samuel hears the voice again and, because of Eli's tutoring, is able to enlarge his perception and come to a more complete understanding of God.

What is unique in this story is not the manner in which Samuel's experience is similar to or different from other mystical experiences, but the way in which Samuel's own interpretive apparatus about God is enlarged. This understanding of religious experience was part of the communal context within which Samuel had his own religious experience. Consequently, Samuel's understanding of this experience (even though the experience was temporal and passive, but not ineffable) became noetic only after Eli's assistance in helping Samuel interpret the experience as an encounter with God. Thus, communities and the relations we build within communities carry the tools which can build the interpretive bonds between our temporal experience and our ultimate ideals.

A second illustration, taken from the life of the Apostle Paul, amplifies this point. In Acts 9, Paul has a mystical encounter with God which fundamentally reorders his life and his understanding and interpretation of the meaning of the religious quest. Traveling to Damascus to further his campaign against the first Christians, Paul is blinded by a light and hears a voice telling him to change his ways and come to a new understanding and interpretation of the nature of the religious life.

The important element in this experience is that it does not alter Paul's inherent Jewishness. It alters the way in which Paul centers the purpose of his life around a new understanding of the will of God.[371] This experience did not lead Paul off in an entirely unknown direction, but altered his understanding and interpretation of the intentions of God and the value of non-Jews in God's ultimate purposes.

Both examples are cited to suggest that within specific religious traditions religious experiences are understood and interpreted along lines which extend interpretations of their particular religious traditions. Both examples emphasize the perceptual and interpretive shift which must occur in order to see reality accurately beyond the pre-defined limits of one's limited personal consciousness. In neither case could the established conceptual apparatus handle the new experience, but, through a perceptual and interpretive shift, new conceptions were created which could bring illumination and understanding to these new experiences.

This brief overview is meant to suggest that the dominant element in religion is not the unique qualities of individual religious experience spread across various religious traditions, but the contextualization of individual religious experience within each specific tradition and community. Religious experience, moreover, is an historical entity giving rise to an ultimate interpretation. In each religious tradition, a specific understanding of religious experience is mediated through the community.

In a helpful article on the role each religious context plays on one's understanding of religious experience, Robert Gimello writes,

> [religious experience] is inextricably bound up with, dependent upon and usually subservient to the deeper beliefs and values of the traditions, cultures, and historical milieu which harbour it. As it is intricately related to those beliefs and values, so

---

[371] Segal, Alan. <u>Paul the Convert: the Apostalate and Apostasy of Saul the Pharisee.</u> New Haven, CN: Yale University Press, 1987.

must it vary according to them.[372]

Elsewhere, Gimello argues that it is not only impossible, but also quite artificial to try to reduce the variety of religious experiences to a vital common core.[373] By contrast, all religious traditions illustrate that religious experiences within their tradition have specific structures formed from concepts, beliefs, values and expectations built into the very fabric of a specific religious tradition.[374] They are structured this way because they reflect the way in which the overall interpretive meaning of this tradition is communicated.

Combined with this specific understanding of religious experience mediated by various religious traditions is the belief that no religious experience gains ultimate meaning without some form of mediation. We need ideas and rituals which build 'felt unities.' These 'felt unities' are the bonds created by interpretation which mediate between our lived experience and our ultimate ideal. These 'felt unities,' moreover, retain their strength in connecting the historical with the eternal provided they remain plausible in their explanation of our lived reality.

Schleiermacher, for example, suggests that an individual has pre-reflective experiences which acquire cognitive meaning through the interpretive role of the religious community. Despite various criticisms of this line of argument,[375] there are plenty of sources to support the notion that we have experiences which go beyond our capacity to understand them. What Schleiermacher has noticed, however, is the fact that these experiences become intelligible only when set within a religious context which, by interpreting these experiences, provides meaning and understanding. These interpretations become the heavenly bonds which connect our contingent experience with our ultimate religious ideal.

Earlier, it was noted that William James had included 'immediacy' as one

---

[372] Robert M. Gimello, "Mysticism in Its Contexts," Mysticism and Religious Traditions. Edited by Steven T. Katz. New York: Oxford University Press, 1983, p. 63.
[373] Ibid., p. 62.
[374] Ibid., pp. 60-65.
[375] Wayne Proudfoot's Religious Experience, Berkeley, CA: The University of California Press, 1985, is one notable example.

of the four elements distinguishing religious experience.[376]   This emphasis, however, captured only the initial experience and not the whole event. The whole event includes why humans have experiences they consider religious and what these experiences are supposed to mean. It is in the preparation for and reflection upon religious experience that so many other dimensions of knowledge and interpretation come into play.

Hans Penner amplifies this point when he writes,

> If [religious] experiences have any significance it will be necessary to locate these experiences within the set of relations which mediate them.[377]

This is not to suggest that one does not have an experience one interprets as 'immediate.' Such an interpretation of 'immediacy' will fail to produce contact with the overarching ideal in which these contingent experiences have their ultimate value.

The effort in recent years to find a common core to religious experience and to connect the varieties of religious traditions found throughout the world to this common core has obscured the important and primary role the religious community plays in producing contact with a realm possessing an overarching ideal. Although the explanatory hypothesis offered by some philosophers of religion has proven useful,[378] it has often overlooked the vital role the religious community plays in providing the mediating links between why people desire a religious interpretation of reality and how this interpretation sustains them in their life.[379]

In the process, the unique features and experiences within each religious tradition are ignored in order to find points of contact compatible across religious lines whether or not these points of contact actually transport one into contact

---

[376] James, Wm. op. cit., pp. 292-293.

[377] Hans Penner, "The Mystical Illusion," Katz, loc. cit., p. 98.

[378] Hick, John. op. cit.

[379] Toward a Universal Theology of Religion, edited by Leonard Swidler and No Other Name? by Paul Knitter are two of several other sources which substantiate this observation.

with an ultimate ideal which makes sense of one's life. Enlarging on this point, Steven Katz observes,

> The Christian experience of unio mystica (mystical union) fulfilled in Christ is not the Buddhist experience of nirvana. The Buddhist is 'nirvanized' i.e. become a new ontic reality in which there is no place for either individual souls or a transcendent Divine Being...Karma not grace governs the movement of the historic-transcendental situation and necessity rather than a benevolent will provides the causal power.[380]

Robert Corrington amplifies this point when he makes a case for the interpretive role played by one's relation to one's community. It is within communities that signs and symbols are appropriated, reviewed, and rejected or embraced on the basis of their ability to facilitate an individual's acquisition of meaning and understanding. Subsequently, signs and symbols play an indispensable role in the understanding and interpretation of lived experience. Signs and symbols form the bridge that links one's life as a discontinuous bundle of multiple experiences with an interpretive framework which provides unity and meaning.[381]

This is not to deny the reality of the individual dimension in religious experience. It is simply an attempt to show that there is more to religious experience than an individual's experience of it. Individual religious experience is meant to be an awakening to a reality that is often elusive. It is in this awakening that the odyssey for an overarching ideal begins. The community, as the repository of this ideal, fundamentally shapes one's understanding of these experiences and provides the signs and symbols which make it possible to move from seeing life as a series of isolated individual experiences to seeing the coherent meaning behind all of life's experiences.

What these contemporary developments illustrate is the key role played by the religious community which was recognized by both Schleiermacher and

---

[380] Steven Katz, "The 'Conservative' Character of Mystical Experience," Katz, op. cit., pp. 40-41.
[381] Corrington, Robert S. The Community of Interpreters. Macon, GA: Mercer University Press, 1987.

Royce. These recent developments reinforce the thesis of this paper that interpretation of individual experience is only meaningful when anchored to community. Since interpretation and community are inextricably linked, the interpretive role of the religious community in Schleiermacher and Royce will now be considered.

Section III. The Interpretive Role of the Religious Community in Schleiermacher and Royce

Chapter Six

The Interpretive Role of the Religious Community in Schleiermacher

In Schleiermacher, one finds a developed understanding of the interpretive role of the religious community. Schleiermacher begins by noting that in order to define the essence of Christianity, which he feels must be done, one must separate the permanently identical from the changeable elements within Christianity, or any other manifestation of religious faith for that matter.[382] Because one's religious consciousness is subject to variation, one must determine the common element in all diverse expressions of religious faith. Religious faith, moreover, is cultivated and perpetuated by expressions of piety contextualized in particular religious communities.

The Role of Piety

Schleiermacher specifically states that piety, which is the primary feeling or experience giving rise to religious communities, is the consciousness of being absolutely dependent or being in relation with God.[383]   This feeling or consciousness of being absolutely dependent on God is not an accidental element subject to specific people and to variation and change, but is a universal element conditioning all of life.   This awareness or consciousness, moreover, is not determined rationally, but develops experientially as one becomes aware of the meaning of this reality through the mediating influence of the religious

---

[382] Schleiermacher, F. The Christian Faith. p. 4, #2.2.
[383] Ibid., p. 12, #4.

community.[384]

The themes of coherence and contingency reflect the way in which Schleiermacher develops his understanding of the role of the religious community in the interpretation of religious experience. Since piety is an expression of the form of religious experience contextualized within the religious community, the expression of piety is both a reflection of a particular form of religious consciousness and a reflection of a particular religious community.[385]

Piety, as a form of religious experience, is feeling. Feeling is immediate and self-referential in contrast to knowing and doing, which are externally oriented and contextual. Religious experience, or feeling, is a combination of one's self-consciousness exercising a reciprocity between receptivity in one's response to God and spontaneity in one's action towards the world and other humans.

This form of religious experience gives rise to the feeling of absolute dependence which can only arise from an encounter with God. The feeling of absolute dependence is both a self-consciousness which accompanies all one's activities and a consciousness that all spontaneous activities originate from a source outside of oneself. That is to say, there is no self-constituting ego unencumbered by social connections. In the feeling of absolute dependence one is aware of the self and the world in its relationship to God.[386]

In the feeling of absolute dependence one experiences the presence of God as grace. The need for grace arises from the development within one's consciousness of the reality of sin. When such consciousness awakens one becomes aware of the mediation of grace through the person of Jesus of Nazareth.[387] One's relationship to the consciousness of Jesus is only possible through one's participation in the Christian religious community. Thus, the religious community plays the mediating role in bringing an individual whose religious consciousness has been awakened to sin into living contact with the

---

[384] Ibid., p. 133, #33.
[385] Ibid., p. 6 #3.2; Highlighted recently in such works as, Klemm, David. Hermeneutical Inquiry: Volume II. Atlanta, GA: Scholar's Press, 1986.
[386] Ibid., p. 8,#3.
[387]ibid., p. 52, #11.

God-consciousness of Jesus Christ which mediates redemption from sin through grace.

Schleiermacher amplifies this reality by noting that in any actual conscious state, the human is aware of both an unchanging identity, which has been defined as the coherent, continuous element, and the changing determination of our environment, which has been defined as the contingent, fluctuating element.[388]   Together, coherence and contingency reflect both an objective, changeless representation of who and what one is and a subjective, changing representation of what and how one experiences.

The Role of the Religious and Sensible Self-Consciousness

Pivotal to Schleiermacher's presentation of the emergence of piety and the experience of one's absolute dependence on God is the recognition that there is a highest consciousness which he defines as the religious self-consciousness and a lower consciousness which he defines as the sensible self-consciousness. These two aspects of one's human consciousness define both a self-identical element, which is typified by an unwavering sense of one's absolute dependence on God and a changing element typified by one's sense of a continually wavering experience of life.[389]

To hold these two elements together one needs the mediating bonds of the religious community. In fact, if it is impossible for the higher religious self-consciousness to exist in relationship to the lower sensible self-consciousness then it would be impossible to have either an experience of the feeling of absolute dependence on God or have this feeling appear in time. The two levels of consciousness are not joined in a particular moment, but co-exist in a reciprocal relationship within the same moment. Thus, through the relation of the higher religious self-consciousness and the lower sensible self-consciousness, the reciprocal relation between the coherent, continuous element of our consciousness exists simultaneously with the contingent, changing element of our consciousness.

---

[388] Ibid., p. 12, #4.1.
[389] Ibid., p. 21, #5.3.

The sensible self-consciousness is constituted by a series of moments with differing content and reflect how one's relationships with other human beings is time-bound and temporal. The influence of others on one is likewise time-bound and temporal. The feeling of absolute dependence, on the other hand, is changeless, always the same. It is self-identical, consistent over time, and does not evoke a series of clearly distinct moments which are distinguishable from one another. As a result, the higher religious consciousness where one is aware of their absolute dependence on God must become joined to the various manifestations of the sensible self-consciousness through the church.

The sensible self-consciousness is a consciousness of partial feelings of freedom and dependence. Human self-consciousness is constituted by the fluctuating exchange between these two poles. The feeling of absolute dependence, on the other hand, is the same in every moment of consciousness. What changes in one's moment of consciousness is not one's feeling of absolute dependence, but a recognition that this feeling is understood differently because of the different ways this feeling is interpreted within sensible self-consciousness.[390]

Thus, one's understanding of the higher self-consciousness is a recognition that it is here that one experiences the unifying principle of life. By contrast, one's understanding of the sensible self-consciousness is that a unifying principle must be found in order to bind the contingency of the fluctuating, time-bound experiences of life into a meaningful whole.[391] Together, one recognizes a need to find a unifying bond which can provide the coherent, ultimate meaning of life.[392] Thus, Schleiermacher can write that every religious faith, expressed through its religious community, is both an external, objective unity which reflects its definite beginning and continuity over time, and an internal, subjective unity which identifies the particular modifications the religious community has undergone in developing its general character both in relation to all other religious communities and in relation to its own historical interpretations of religious experience.[393]

---

[390] Ibid., p. 22, #5.4.
[391] Ibid., p. 23, #5.4.
[392] Ibid., p. 40, #9.1.
[393] Ibid., p. 44, #10.

Every religious community exists to embody an ideal. If the ideal is not sustained by the community it will die. Thus, the two-fold task of the religious thinker is to define the unique essence of Christianity which provides the coherent building ideal that can unify all contingent elements of the historical, particular religious communities and the way in which these reflect the contingencies of individual existence.[394] This coherent building ideal is further defined as that which remains constant throughout the most diverse expressions of religious affection within the same religious understanding while being absent from analogous affections within other religious communities.[395]

The common core element that all Christians have in mind when they speak of the development of their religious consciousness is identity with the person and work of Jesus Christ. The expression of a Christian religious consciousness differs vastly throughout the various expressions of Christianity worldwide. Nevertheless, all Christians trace the origin of their religious faith and the development of their unique form of religious consciousness back to Christ and the religious community which originated through him.[396] Thus, within Christianity, the religious consciousness is seeking for redemption through the unifying ideal revealed through the influence of the God-consciousness of Jesus Christ. The church, as the human institution of this ideal, exists solely to preserve and propagate this understanding of Christ's redeeming influence and activity.[397]

For the Christian, moreover, the common unifying thread drawing all into religious community is the love of Christ.[398] This love of Christ both binds Christians together in community and provides the spirit which makes interpretation of this ideal possible. This common community spirit develops as those so bound determine to seek the advancement and good of the religious community.

Schleiermacher extends his theme of the way in which the religious community transmits the timeless influence of Jesus' God-consciousness in

---

[394] Ibid., p. 53, #11.1.
[395] Ibid., p. 54, #11.1.
[396] Ibid., p. 54, #11.2.
[397] Ibid., p. 57, #11.4.
[398] Ibid., p. 562, #121.1.

history. In one telling proposition, Schleiermacher writes,

> The fellowship of believers, animated by the Holy Spirit, remains ever self-identical in its attitude to Christ and to this spirit (coherence theme), but in its relation to the world it is subject to change and variation (contingency theme).

Schleiermacher continues by emphasizing the necessity of the church, as an historical body, expressing itself in a form whereby its timeless element is able to be expressed in each new generation while finding the appropriate mode for each new generation in which to express this timeless element. In other words, there is a timeless message of Christianity anchored in the redemption accomplished by Jesus of Nazareth and a time-bound element in which each new generation must determine the best format for presenting this message of redemption to their period of history.[399]

The continuous and coherent aspects of the church's presentation form the ideals which preserve the church's mediation of the Holy Spirit. The church, thus, becomes not only the embodiment of the spirit of Christ's God-consciousness, but also the way in which this spirit is preserved and transmitted to each subsequent generation.[400]

By contrast, the changing and contingent element in the religious community is not determined by the common spirit of the church, but by human nature. As such, it reflects the understanding that every timeless element must become time-bound if it is to influence human consciousness. In the process of becoming time-bound, it fundamentally constrains the timeless element to particular forms of presentation.

This changing and contingent element accounts for the vast array of religious communions within the Christian church. The Christian church, as both the coherent and contingent center of Christianity, transmits the changeless message of Christianity through the changing context of particular times and cultures. Is it any wonder, then, that Christian churches take on the peculiar

---

[399] Ibid., p. 582, #126.
[400] Ibid., p. 583, #126.1.

characteristics of the countries in which they reside?. Every embodiment of the religious community is going to reflect the attitudes, opinions and cultures of the country in which it originates.

But this reflection does not dismiss the timeless element of Christianity tied directly to one's understanding of the person and work of Jesus of Nazareth.[401] One must contextualize Christianity in history, otherwise, one fails to recognize the sign producing character of historic contingencies.[402]

To amplify his point, Schleiermacher divides his subsequent treatment of the church into the coherent element and the contingent element and treats each element separately. He begins with a treatment of the essential and invariable features of the church.

The Role of the Essential Features of the Church

The Christian religious community retains its unique self-identity by bearing exclusive and enduring witness to Christ through Scripture, preaching, and rituals. Self-identity mediated by the community is realized in the individual through the individual's identity with the whole through prayer.[403] Thus, prayer is a bond-building activity in which individual attention is directed to the consciousness mediated by the community.

Because the Christian religious community exists to bear witness to Christ it is illogical, if not impossible, for the Christian religious community to exist for any other purpose. When it loses this purpose, as its integrating ideal, it will lose its reason for existence and cease to have relevance as a presentation of the God-consciousness of Jesus Christ. To lose contact with the presentation and perpetuation of the God-consciousness of Jesus Christ is to cease to have living fellowship with the community and its Lord. Such disruption of our living fellowship with Christ leads to a rupture in one's timeless, coherent contact with the redemptive influence of a unifying ideal mediated as the God-consciousness

---

[401] Sung Min Park has demonstrated this element in his unpublished dissertation cited earlier.

[402] Ibid., p. 585, #126.2.

[403] Christian Faith, p. 586, #127.

of Jesus Christ.

In bearing legitimate witness to the person and work of Christ, the Christian religious community helps to discern what is timeless from what is time bound. This is an essential distinction. The timeless message of the redemption accomplished by Jesus of Nazareth must be preserved from corruption. In every generation, threats to the purity of this presentation develop because of the encroachment of the world on the Christian religious consciousness.

This tension has existed since the days of the Apostles. The Apostles had the direct influence of Christ in their apprehension of the Christian religious consciousness. Christians today do not. Nevertheless, the Christian religious community has perpetuated the influence of Christ through its perpetuation of the Apostolic understanding of Christian religious consciousness in the church.[404]

This understanding has formed *both* the direct influence of Christ *and* the interpretation of this life by the Apostles and the Early Church. The Apostolic Church reflects more than merely various interpretations of the person and work of Christ. It was the combined consciousness of the disciples making their response to Jesus and the influence of his consciousness upon them through interpretation which formed the earliest Christian consciousness.[405]

In outlining this influence by Jesus on the Early Church, Schleiermacher emphasizes that the original activity of Christ left an oral and written tradition which was identical. The written tradition now stands alone as a static embodiment of the dynamic oral tradition. Preaching from the written tradition awakens the truth distilled from the oral tradition in written form. This activity of preaching remains the way in which the church continually renews itself and perpetuates its ongoing connection with the historic witness of Jesus Christ.[406]

---

[404] Ibid., p. 587, #127.2.

[405] Ibid., p. 588, #127.2.

[406] In many respects the theory Schleiermacher advances regarding the role of preaching in the preservation and perpetuation of the Christian religious community is similar to the emphasis Jurgen Habermas advances in his two volume work on the theory of communicative action. Habermas' treatment of speech-acts deriving meaning from their context in specific communities parallels Schleiermacher. Both resemble the work of Wittgenstein and his treatment of language games and the way in which specific rules in language make sense because of their specific context. See, Habermas, Jurgen. The Theory of Communicative Action, vol. I, II. Boston, MA: Beacon Press, 1981, translated in 1987.

The Role of Scripture

In defining the difference between accepting the authority of Scripture in its presentation of Christ and affirming one's faith in Christ, Schleiermacher makes it clear that one must have faith in Christ before the authority of Scripture makes sense.[407] Schleiermacher clearly believes the authority of Scripture cannot be derived from reason alone. He rejects, moreover, basing one's religious faith in God and one's confidence in holy Scripture on reason alone for to do so would leave religious faith only for the most refined intellects and would not reflect the true nature of Christianity which originated with the first disciples.[408] Christian faith must be universally accessible and universally the same. Christian faith can change neither in its method of appropriation nor in the manner in which one gains access to its message.

The role of Scripture in faith remains critical. Schleiermacher is careful to distinguish Scripture's authority from its role as the first expression of the faith as well as the standard against which all subsequent presentations of the faith are measured.[409] The Scriptures both preserve the Early Church's understanding of Jesus and correct any deviant presentations of Jesus which would corrupt the influence of his common spirit upon the Christian religious community and its participants.

In his treatment of Scripture and its proper understanding and interpretation, Schleiermacher continues to distance himself from his contemporaries. In establishing the way in which Scripture shapes religious faith, Schleiermacher states,

> ...in the vocational life of the Apostles the whole activity of the common Spirit ruling in the church approximated as closely as possible to the person-forming union of the Divine Essence with human nature which constituted the person of Christ and that only in this light can what is outward in the actions of the Apostles be regarded as partially

---

[407] Ibid., p. 591, #128.
[408] Ibid., p. 592, #128
[409] Ibid., p. 594, #129.

> different in origin from the inward it was meant to express. This being assumed, it at once follows that we must reject the suggestions that in virtue of their divine inspiration the sacred books demand a hermeneutical and critical treatment different from one guided by the rules that obtain elsewhere...a pure and complete apprehension of the various aspects of Christ's life is an essential precondition of the Apostles' official action as a whole...different people interpreted Christ's life and work in different ways.[410]

Because Christ's life and work could be presented in different ways, it became essential to distill the essential memories regarding Christ and his teachings which could lead one into the Kingdom of God.

In presenting the Scriptures, moreover, Schleiermacher distinguishes between doctrinal books and historical books. Doctrinal books were meant to bear upon the actual circumstances of Christian people, so that the interpretation by the Apostles could form the dominant ideas and purposes of the believers. The historical books, on the other hand, were meant simply to rehearse the similarly influential words and deeds of Christ and the Apostles.[411] Together, both the doctrinal and the historical books were intended to become the source of regulating all thinking regarding the Christian religious consciousness. As such, they were meant to direct the human mind to the essence of the message beyond its time-bound form.

Each age must interpret the Scriptures in accordance with its time and place. Christian orthodoxy is defined anew in each age by the manner in which the church teaches, as it transmits, the meaning and purpose of Christ and the Apostles' teaching. This transmission, moreover, permits the coherence of the unifying message of the Christian-consciousness to be preserved while adapting its presentation to reflect each new contingent reality.

---

[410] Ibid., p. 600, #130.2,3. Contemporary biblical scholars as respected as Raymond Brown amplify this same point. See, Brown, Raymond E. and John P Meier. Antioch and Rome. New York: Paulist Press, 1983, which deals with four different understandings of Jesus and the church as reflected in the teachings of the four gospels.
[411] Ibid.,p. 606, #131.2.

The Role of Preaching

One gains access to the message of Christian faith by preaching. Because the faith of the first disciples sprang from the preaching of Jesus, so must our faith spring from the preaching of Jesus. Preaching, therefore, must recreate the same impact on a contemporary congregation as the original words of Jesus had on his followers. To attain faith, therefore, one's focus must be on the primary method espoused by Jesus and not by the method espoused by the Enlightenment philosophers who sought a faith sustained by reason alone.

Equally problematic, however, are the people who insist on basing their faith on experience alone. Such experience, without the interpretation of experience, renders the proper use of reason obsolete in its ability to help one understand and interpret the nature of religious faith.[412] Together, however, reason and experience provide necessary elements for the interpretive process in order to provide meaning and understanding for our faith. Reason helps to construct scientific understanding of the nature of faith while experience helps to fill the empty shell of scientific understanding with concrete, historical embodiments of such faith. Through interpretation, reason and experience are synthesized into a meaningful whole.

Preaching preserves the meaning of the gospel by presenting a timeless message in a time-bound form. Preaching in every age recreates the preaching of Jesus. As such, it perpetuates a timeless example and transmits a timeless message. But preaching must be continually renewed. Preaching develops in different forms and different modes to present itself in different times and places.[413]

Preaching, moreover, ministers to those for whom the Christian message has relevance and receptivity.[414] Preaching also exhibits an uneven receptivity among the listening audience. As suggested earlier, Schleiermacher attributed this uneven receptivity to the stage of development of the individual. He extends this

---

[412] Ibid.,p. 594, #128.3.
[413] Ibid., p. 611, #132.
[414] Ibid., p. 611, #133.

idea by stating that the source of preachers should come from those who have lived with a well developed feeling of absolute dependence and can transmit the vitality of this experience and feeling to those who desire this vitality, but have yet to experience it. Thus, true preachers are ones who have developed bonds within the divine realm and can, through interpretation, lead a person into this realm.

The Christian religious community can only continue to exist if the strong transmit their experience of God and their understanding of Christ to the weak. This communication takes place through a variety of forms, but is chiefly expressed through preaching and the interpretive role of the religious community in presenting its ideas through preaching. This pattern of communication has several distinct features, but is characterized by its adherence to the rigorous standard of presenting the view of Christ as given in Scripture.[415]

The individuals selected to preach in the Christian religious community are chosen on the condition that they live with a feeling of absolute dependence and exhibit giftedness in presenting this feeling to others.[416] Preaching, moreover, must take place in the church and the church must be ordered in such a way so as to permit such preaching to occur. To ensure such preaching, Schleiermacher advocates a parallel organization to the church which emerges for the specific function of developing expert interpretation of Scripture and to bring it to full expression through the life and ministry of the church.[417]

The Role of the Sacraments

The person and work of Christ sets the tone for the message which the Christian religious community transmits throughout its history. Thus, in the preservation of its communal identity, the Christian religious community also promotes the practice of religious rituals which capture the original spirit of the God-consciousness of Jesus Christ. Thus, within the Protestant Christian

---

[415] Ibid., p. 613, #133.1.

[416] Ibid., p. 616, #134.2.

[417] Ibid., p. 619, #135.2.

128

community one finds the emergence of two Christian sacraments.[418] As noted, these sacraments are identified as sacraments because they reflect and capture the God-consciousness of Jesus Christ in forms which can be transmitted to subsequent generations. In other words, they are signs which have a temporal embodiment which, when practiced in the church, can elevate one to the eternal spirit with which they are connected. They are the signs which mediate between human nature and God. These two sacraments so identified are Baptism and the Lord's Supper.

Baptism

Baptism is given by Christ to inaugurate a continuous, conscious awareness of one's ongoing fellowship with Christ. It is not essential how it is done, but it is essential that something is done. Schleiermacher interprets the role of baptism as an act initiated by Christ and perpetuated by the first disciples. It is impossible to know how they performed this ritual exactly, but the outward form is not of essential importance. What is of essential importance is that some form of baptism be undertaken in order to ensure continuity with the person and work of Jesus.[419] Thus, baptism is a sign which, when interpreted properly, leads one into conscious unity with the body of Christ.

Schleiermacher shows his Reformed roots in advocating baptism's role in the coherent structure of the religious community. Specifically, he challenges those Christian religious groups, like the Quakers, who have labeled water baptism superfluous to Christian faith, to come up with another sacrament which connects the individual to the community in the same dramatic way.[420] What is essential to Schleiermacher is that one determine that the external action be in sync with the internal intention. Baptism must be seen as the ultimate expression of an individual to be identified with the Christian religious community which expresses the spirit of Christ.[421] Baptism must be an expression of one's faith.[422]

---

[418] Ibid., p. 588, #127.2.
[419] Ibid., p. 619, #136.
[420] Ibid., p. 624, #136.
[421] ibid., p. 628, #137.1.

Thus, infant baptism is only completed when one is confirmed into the Christian religious community by a profession of faith.[423] Baptism is a historical sign which must be interpreted in order to have meaning. Thus, The goal of infant baptism is to help begin the development of a Christian religious consciousness which can impact the individual in such a way that it starts them on the road to a full affirmation and profession of one's faith. Without this as the ultimate goal, infant baptism becomes an inadequate substitute for introducing one into the religious consciousness of the Christian community.

The Lord's Supper

The Lord's Supper symbolizes the nature of the Christian's ongoing living fellowship with Christ. The Lord's Supper, as the second Christian sacrament, is given to sustain the individual in his or her identification and imitation of Christ. The Lord's Supper would be unnecessary if the confession of faith at one's entrance into Christian religious consciousness sustained itself unwaveringly. But it does not. As a result, one must return continually to an identification with the life of Christ through participation in the Lord's Supper as the symbol of identification with the person and work of Christ.

At the core of the controversy is the various interpretations given the words of Christ. Therefore, it is of the utmost importance to establish the meaning of Christ's words and how they bear on participants in the various expressions of the Christian religious community. Schleiermacher rejects both the Roman Catholic and the Quaker understanding of the sacraments on this count.

He rejects the Roman Catholic understanding on the basis that it advances magical effects which cannot be substantiated by Scripture.[424] He rejects the Quaker understanding on the premise that they deny any spiritual effect to participation in the physical elements of the sacraments. Both groups fail to

---

[422] This is an interesting position for Schleiermacher to promote given his contextualization in the Reformed Church at the time. Clearly, he is advocating more than his superiors in the Reformed Church would embrace and seems to advocate a position more closely akin to the Anabaptists then to his own Reformed denomination.
[423] Ibid., p. 633, #138.
[424] Ibid., p. 646, #140.2.

recognize the benefit and the limit Christ places on the institution of the sacraments. The benefit is to derive a spiritual effect from a historical activity. The limit is to ascribe only this spiritual benefit which reflects Christ's prescription for it.[425]   Thus, in advocating the perpetuation of physical participation in the Lord's Supper, Schleiermacher advocates that the continuity of the Lord's Supper is necessary in order to maintain a mediating sign which can preserve contact with the timeless ideal of the Christian religious community.[426] Together, Baptism and the Lord's Supper identify the beginning of one's conscious relationship with Christ and the ongoing relationship one is meant to enjoy with Christ through the religious community.[427]

The Role of Prayer

Prayer, although not a sacrament, functions much like a sacrament in connecting the individual's religious consciousness with the God-consciousness of Jesus Christ. Prayer expresses intentionality of consciousness in the religious person. As such, it creates a heavenly bond between what one needs and desires and how the God-consciousness of Jesus Christ will shape the satisfaction of these needs and desires. Without prayer, it would be impossible to understand either the full nature of the Christian life or make any progress in obtaining a deeper understanding of the God-consciousness of Jesus Christ.   Through prayer, individuals gather together to practice a common religious action which in turn gives rise to a common religious consciousness.[428]   This common action creates bonds between individuals and shapes these bonds into a common form which can lay hold of all participants equally. By laying hold of all participants equally, the heavenly bonds contextualized in the historical church are able to provide a modification of individual religious consciousness in order to bring the individual into an apprehension of the will of God.[429]   One does not influence

---

[425] Ibid., p. 647, #140.3.
[426] Ibid., pp. 649-650, #140.4.
[427] Ibid., p. 589, #127.3.
[428] Ibid., p. 671, #146.1.
[429] Ibid., p. 672, #147.1.

God's will through prayer, one comes to understand the nature of the religious life through prayer. As a result, prayer works to bring one's individual religious consciousness into alignment with the communal religious consciousness and, together, to understand the will of God.

Prayer reflects an inner state with an outer influence. The inner attitude which gives rise to prayer helps produce the outer circumstances which make the meaning of this prayer possible.[430] Prayer is only effective when one is active in fulfilling what prayer has made apparent to one, and this is the Christian vocation.

The Role of Christian Worship

Preaching, Scripture reading, Baptism, the Lord's Supper, and Prayer are all all aspects of Christian worship. Christian worship as such is the interlude between lonely contemplation with Christ and one's common, active life as the citizen of a state. Christian worship is communal and public. It is a withdrawal from one's active common life to join with others in celebration and stimulation of one's Christian religious consciousness.[431] Through Christian worship, both an individual's response to Christ and the religious community's presentation of the life of Christ are joined. The way in which Christian worship is practiced, therefore, fundamentally reflects the Christian religious consciousness of which one is a part.

On the one hand, it is unfortunate that no clear unity regarding the practices of Christian worship have prevailed. On the other hand, this very reality reflects the common theme of coherence and contingency which now compels attention. The coherent aspect of the Christian religious consciousness is perpetuated by participation in the collective practices of every Christian religious community. The contingent aspect of the Christian religious consciousness is preserved through the various expressions each activity assumes in the variety of Christian religious communities throughout the world.[432]

---

[430] Ibid., p. 674, #147.2.
[431] Ibid., p. 639, #139.1.
[432] Ibid., p. 642, #139.3.

The unity of the Christian religious community is predicated on the participation of all individuals in the God-consciousness of Jesus Christ. Such participation, moreover, arises from deliberate identification and interpretation of the activities of Jesus. This identification and interpretation connects the Christian religious community with the continuing influence of Christ in each new age.[433]

The Coherence Producing Role of the Church

The goal of all of these practices is to bring the individual into living fellowship with Christ through the ministry of the church.[434] Through the ministry of the church, moreover, every individual connects with the common spirit of the church typified as the spirit of Christ. Ideally, every member who identifies with the Christian religious community does so because of his or her accurate interpretation of utterances and impulses originating from the spirit of Christ. Such interpretation demonstrates one's identity with the spirit of the community and indicates an individual's willingness to give free assent to the decisions of the community as legitimate manifestations of the spirit of Christ.

The common spirit of Christ is timeless, but its manifestation develops across time through history. In like manner, the common spirit of Christ impacts the individual with its timeless content, but develops within the individual religious consciousness in a time-bound and historical way. As a result, the development of Christ-consciousness within individual religious consciousness captures the way in which the coherent message of the common spirit of the church takes root in and through the contingent development in the individual religious consciousness.[435]

Coupled with the development of individual religious consciousness in relation to communal consciousness is the way in which the Christian religious community regulates what will be included and what will be jettisoned in its

---

[433] Ibid., p. 590, #127.3.
[434] Ibid., p. 660, ##144.1.
[435] Ibid., pp. 661-662, #144.2.

transmission of religious faith. The first order regulation pertains to the way in which one not only perpetuates the life of Christ through preaching, but also interprets this life to daily application in an age far removed from the time of Christ.[436]

Regulation also implies discipline and Schleiermacher is careful to note that under no circumstances should one be fully excommunicated from the church. To excommunicate one from the church is to remove the influence of the God-consciousness of Jesus Christ which the individual needs in order to be restored to the community. The result of excommunication is the complete destruction of the individual's religious consciousness.[437]

The goal of the Christian religious community is to combine individual religious consciousness with communal religious consciousness in formation of the most faithful likeness of the spirit of Christ.[438] Clearly, the church as the Christian religious community does not reflect the spirit of Christ perfectly. But this does not remove the church from its responsibility of pursuing such perfection vigilantly.

The Role of the Church in the World

The contingent element of the Christian religious community is a result of its relationship with the world. The historic distinction of the visible and invisible church is a result of the church's connection with the world.[439] The visible church must co-exist with the world. The church, as a visible institution, is vulnerable to the incursion of the world on its communal consciousness. The co-existence of the world with the church makes the awareness and reality of sin in the church real.

[436] Ibid., p. 666, #145.1.

[437] Ibid., p. 668, #145.2.

[438] Ibid., p. 670, #146.

[439] Ibid., p. 676, #148. The presentation by Augustine of the visible and invisible church exercised a clear influence on Schleiermacher. This classic distinction gave expression to the reality that some individuals within the visible church had not yet embraced or realized the essence of the Christian religious consciousness set forth in speech. Here, Schleiermacher extends this classic teaching by contextualizing its reality within the contingent manifestation of the Christian religious community.

The invisible church, by contrast, is the total effect of the common spirit of the church on the true adherents who express full confidence in the Christian religious consciousness.[440] Thus, those who embrace the Christian ideal of life enter into membership in the invisible church. Schleiermacher claims that the invisible church was never Christ's original intention since Christ's hope was that his redemptive influence would be self-sustaining within individual religious consciousness. In recognition of the fundamental need for historic embodiment, however, the Christian religious community developed as a manifestation in finite form of the universal common spirit of Christ. As the visible embodiment of an invisible ideal it remains imperfect. Nevertheless, it is the vehicle through which Christ's common consciousness anchored to the church is made manifest and accessible in history.

A further distinction between the visible and the invisible church follows our theme of coherence and contingency. The visible church remains the contingent embodiment of the common spirit of Christ within the religious community. The invisible church, by contrast, represents the coherent and timeless realization of the ultimate ideal of the Christian life coming to reside within the particular religious consciousness of every follower of Christ.[441]

The person who is in the process of being redeemed by Christ's redemptive influence is part of the invisible fellowship. This invisible fellowship is not isolated from the visible church, but is joined to it. As a result, the visible and invisible exist in unity with one another. It must be this way, otherwise there would be no historic and time-bound form in which the invisible ideal could be mediated by a visible reality.

Schleiermacher amplifies this position further when he notes the invisible church is the church universal and essentially one, while the visible church is the particular church involved in a multiplicity of divisions and separations.[442] The invisible church lacks any definite form. Its members are related directly by the individual religious consciousness which each individual has developed.

---

[440] ibid., p. 677, #148.1.
[441] Ibid., p. 678, #149.
[442] Ibid., p. 680, #149.2.

Membership consists of those who share similar understandings of the common spirit of Christ present in the Christian religious community. The visible form of the church is not only identified by its external communication, but also creates division among manifestations of the Christian religious consciousness in history by these external expressions. Ideas can unite, but they can also divide. In the case of the establishment of external forms of the Christian religious community, ideas unite individuals around a specific understanding of Christ. At the same time, they divide themselves off from all other forms of the common consciousness of Christ through the diversity of expressions of the Christian religious consciousness in history.

Christ's common consciousness is universally accessible. There is no isolating this consciousness to a specific culture and a specific time and place. But with this universal common consciousness comes a multiplicity of culture and time-bound expressions. As a result, the separations which actually occur in the Christian church, although beckoning its individual members to seek unity with one another, reflect the inevitable reality of the historical contingency of human life and religious reality.[443]

In a fashion reminiscent of Royce, Schleiermacher argues that the Christian religious communal consciousness will gradually win out because humans have an inherent need for unity rather than separation. Although he makes this argument in the context of trying to explain the present existence of division, he does not see division as the ultimate desire of God nor the ultimate outcome of one's individual life.[444]

These divisions are ultimately explainable as a result of differences attributed to language and culture. As different languages and cultures develop their own form of the Christian religious communal consciousness, contingent manifestations of the Christian religious community will emerge. But these are

---

[443] Ibid., p. 681, #150. A supplementary source to this presentation is found in Jerry Dawson's work, Friedrich Schleiermacher: The Evolution of A Nationalist, Austin, TX: University of Texas Press, 1966. Here, Dawson makes a strong case for Schleiermacher's gradual awakening to the necessity of communal unity among the German states and demonstrates the way in which Schleiermacher came to understand the power of communities in all realms of life to transmit the ideals common to that particular community.

[444] Ibid., p. 683, #150.2.

only temporary. The ultimate goal of the Christian religious community is a universal church where all members of the visible church are also members of the invisible church in the extension of Christianity throughout the world.

As noted earlier, Schleiermacher also expresses his confidence in the universal appeal of Christianity. Christianity's appeal worldwide is due to its ability to transmit its eternal ideal throughout vast cultures and language groups spread around the world.[445] Thus, Schleiermacher sees loyalty to one's particular expression of Christianity as beneficial for a time, but not for eternity. Thus, every contingent form of Christian religious consciousness is only a transient form which is meant to mediate contact with the one ultimate reality of the universal church.[446]

In amplifying this point, Schleiermacher adds that proselytizing is appropriate when one's main goal is to extend the universal message of Christianity. It is inappropriate when one's goal is simply to expand the borders of one's own church. Thus, in a form reminiscent of Royce's advocacy of loyalty for the sake of loyalty in order to generate universal loyalty, Schleiermacher advocates the promotion of the Christian religious consciousness through Christian religious communities who are all pursuing the ultimate goal of the communion of saints.[447]

Every contingent presentation of the Christian religious consciousness is corrupted in some form and in some way. No contingent doctrine and no contingent tradition can sustain the force of Christian religious consciousness without creating the necessity of development and change among subsequent generations of its members. In the face of such contingent realities, including corruptions of its truth, falsehood must be restrained. First, falsehood must be restrained in individuals by the corporate guidance of the religious community and then in the religious community by the living saints of the community who are part of the invisible church.[448]

In heading off a controversy regarding the time of origin of the Christian

---

[445] Ibid., p. 686, #152.2.
[446] Ibid., p. 686, #152.2.
[447] Ibid., p. 687, #152.2.
[448] Ibid., p. 691, #155.

community Schleiermacher insists that the Christian religious community has existed only since the time of Christ. The desire to link both the origin of the Church and the meaning of Christ's appearing with Old Testament prophecies which purportedly support such developments is spurious. The rationale turns on Schleiermacher's belief that there is no way to derive from the Old Testament texts themselves the interpretation that the New Testament writers attribute to these texts. Moreover, the credibility and reliability of Christ cannot be predicated on the miracles which he performed.[449]

The nature and veracity of faith, by contrast, is supported not on the basis of miracles and the fulfillment of messianic prophecy, but on the ability to produce fellowship-forming activities among its members which meet human needs. One must form heavenly bonds which interpret these contingent needs through contact with an ultimate unifying reality. To rely on miracles or prophecy or special testimonies to establish faith does not produce a unifying bond which can establish the veracity of Christ. One must be aware of a need for Christ in order to identify Christ as the source of satisfaction for this need. The challenge is to demonstrate that human needs are satisfied by entering into the common consciousness of Christ made accessible through the Christian religious community.[450]

This cycle is endless because although each generation makes progress and develops, every new generation must go through the same process of development.[451] Thus, as Christianity spreads across the whole world it must work continually to conquer the consciousness of sin it encounters throughout the world. As it moves throughout the world it continually strives not only to prevent the incursion of worldly elements into its religious consciousness, but also to conquer these elements by integrating them into the Christian religious consciousness transmitted by the church.

---

[449] Ibid., p. 694, #156.2. This line of reasoning runs directly against John Locke's advocacy for the reasonableness of Christianity partially on the basis of the veracity of Christ's miracles and His fulfillment of OT prophecy. See Locke, John. The Reasonableness of Christianity. Edited by I. T. Ramsey. Stanford, CA: Stanford University Press, 1958.

[450] Ibid., p. 71, #14.Post.

[451] Ibid., p. 696, #157.1.

Although Schleiermacher's treatment is compelling it remains contextualized within explicitly religious communities. In order to demonstrate the religious nature of all acts of interpretation within community, a consideration of Royce's treatment of the interpretive role of the religious community will follow.

Chapter Seven

The Religious Nature of Communities of Interpretation in Royce

Royce expands Schleiermacher's treatment of the Christian community to show the way in which every true community operates to generate and sustain a meaningful ideal. Royce's focus is on the need to find a unifying, meaning-making ideal for life through the interpretation of individual experiences. Royce insists that Christianity is not a religion based on revelation, but a religion of interpretation based on reason, historical contingency, ethical reality, and religious experience. Humans do not think, live and act in isolation. Humans always exist, and interpret this existence, within the broader context of which they are a part; a context that is fundamentally social and communal. Thus, reason, history, ethics and experience form the contingent framework within which communities form and interpretations are generated.

The interpretive role of the religious community is fundamentally anchored to the religious traditions which both distill a particular interpretation of life and communicate this interpretation of life to each successive generation. There are two basic approaches one can take in using a religious tradition. The first approach is to insist that the tradition is static and incapable of providing signs for new interpretations. The second approach is to interpret and evaluate one's tradition from the moral, intellectual and experiential lens of contemporary experience. Royce embraces this second approach and justifies his decision on the basis that it reflects the way in which Paul interpreted the significance of the Christ-event for the Early Church.[452]

In interpreting the Christ-event through the intellectual and experiential lens of contemporary experience, Paul identified the most significant aspects of the religious tradition. This interpretive judgment is different from the traditional and historical approaches in which an attempt is made to establish the dominant

---

[452] Linnell, Cady. op. cit., p. 200; cf. with Segal, Alan. Paul the Convert: The Apostolate and Apostasy of Saul the Pharisee. New Haven, CN: Yale University Press, 1990.

beliefs and practices which become universals.[453]

By amplifying the interpretive approach in his religious philosophy, Royce moves beyond Schleiermacher by expressing his conviction that Christianity, in the form of its traditional presentation, is no longer relevant for individuals dominated by the modern mentality.[454]   Nevertheless, Christianity provides the best material, or, currency, for a new interpretation in which an individual's need for salvation and the method by which this salvation can be obtained are known.

Of particular concern for the interpretive role of the religious community are the signs which Royce identified in chapter three as being used by a religious community to identify both an individual's need for salvation and the way in which this need could be met.   In fact, the degree to which religion can meet human needs by providing the all-encompassing universal ideal will be the degree to which religion remains viable.[455]   Thus, Royce's theory of the interpretive role of the religious community is built on the interpretive judgment of the traveler: what must be determined is the value of his old currency as he exchanges it for new currency.   The value of the new currency is gauged by its plausible explanation in identifying the central needs of the human and the way in which the human can meet these needs.   According to Royce, this is the genius of Christianity.

A second aspect of Christianity which makes this understanding of the interpretive role of the religious community so compelling is the versatility Christianity has displayed in remaining relevant to every new human mind set and mentality.   During its vast 2,000 year history Christianity has confronted all kinds of pressures to modify, abandon or retrench with its message.   Yet, Christianity has been able to meet this challenge by modifying its content in order to preserve its essential form.   The versatility and tenacity Christianity has displayed in facing both sources of pressure have helped to secure its place as the enduring religious

---

[453] Ibid., p. 201.

[454] Royce, J. The Problem of Christianity, vol. I, p. 14.

[455] Ibid., p. 385.   Peter Berger makes a similar point when identifying the necessity of plausibility structures and the role religion plays in providing plausible explanations for the world being the way it is. See Berger, Peter. The Sacred Canopy. New York: Doubleday, 1967.

tradition which can handle change.[456]   In creating this tradition of endurance amidst change, Christianity has had a profound influence on the development of religious consciousness.

The Interpretive Role of the Religious Community in the Formation of Religious Consciousness

Earlier, in chapter five, Royce established that religious consciousness develops within community and develops in a progressive pattern.   The development of religious consciousness begins when an individual recognizes both their need for salvation and the religious ideal necessary to obtain it.[457]   This recognition leads one to look for an unifying ideal which can place the past and future in perspective as a communal forming consciousness within the individual. In essence, an individual identifies with the ideal of the community. If this ideal is able to provide an integrating interpretation of one's contingent experiences then it becomes the unifying ideal which saves.[458]

By identifying with a social history shaped by past traditions and future hopes, one enters into communication with other selves who share this same history. Through communication, one's religious consciousness is further shaped by the establishment and perpetuation of a community of discourse.[459]   Through communication, the interpretive process identifies and interprets temporal signs which carry eternal meaning. Thus, the common consciousness of the community transmits its coherence forming ideal to the specific consciousness of the individual and this is its religious task.

In this way, Christian religious consciousness shapes individual religious consciousness by drawing individuals into unity through involvement in and communication of its traditions of participation. For example, as Schleiermacher

---

[456] Ibid., p. 389.

[457] Royce, J. Source of Religious Insight, p. 31.

[458] Oppenheimer, Frank. op. cit., p. 361.

[459] Robert Wuthnow has made a strong case for the way in which the community of discourse establishes the context within which language and communication make sense. See Wuthnow, R. Communities of Discourse. Cambridge, MA: Harvard University Press, 1989.

demonstrated above, the traditions of baptism and the Lord's Supper communicate a common understanding of Christianity which draws each individual into a common communal consciousness. By being drawn into this communal consciousness one's personal religious consciousness is specifically shaped and formed. By cooperation in traditions of participation our religious consciousness is shaped through specific uses of language, customs, traditions and culture. These are both embodiments of communal consciousness and complex signs which convey significance when connected with individual consciousness through interpretation[460]

What Royce has identified is that shared understandings develop in every true from of community. Through cooperation in a variety of areas and at a variety of levels, shared understanding forms. These shared understandings expand Schleiermacher's common heritage and distill an awareness shared by individuals within particular communities. Ultimately, love, as the sustaining quality of a community, is cultivated among each individual member by these rituals of cooperation and this spirit is extended to all the members in the inevitable development of religious consciousness. This kind of love is predicated on loyalty and creates the atmosphere in which a unique religious consciousness can develop within the members of the community.

Earlier, in chapter five, Royce established that the world is fundamentally social and teleological. Thus, the interpretive role of the religious community is central in creating the context within which coherence generating unifying ideals can be communicated in a way which can provide understanding for the contingent experiences of an individual life. Royce grounds his understanding of religious consciousness as social and teleological in the metaphysical nature of the world. Royce writes,

> ...the world is throughout essentially social, as is also our own human world...[461]

But how does one connect with this reality? It is only through the historical,

---

[460] Oppenheimer, Frank. op. cit., p. 362.
[461] Royce, J. The Problem of Christianity, vol. II, p. 374.

contingent elements which are signs worthy of being interpreted. The world is also teleological. The teleological nature of the world influences the way in which signs are interpreted to produce a coherent, unified understanding that provides meaning.

Thus, individual religious consciousness is shaped by both the social and the teleological nature of the world. These two forces combine to elevate individual religious consciousness into communal consciousness where a meaning making interpretation can produce the 'felt unities' introduced by Schleiermacher in chapter two, but never developed. It is these felt unities, created by the interpretive activity of the community, which connect contingent experiences into a coherent whole.[462]   Royce offers numerous examples of how individual consciousness is shaped by communal consciousness: a well-trained chorus, an orchestra, an athletic team, a rowing crew, a committee or the Supreme Court are all examples of the way in which individuals are joined in community through the interpretation of signs.[463]   These examples reflect the way in which Royce believes a communal ideal can galvanize individual interests into a meaningful whole. Without these communal ideals, consciousness remains disconnected. Universal ideals, contextualized in a specific communal consciousness, shape individual consciousness.

Moral behavior is one example of how communal consciousness shapes individual consciousness. Royce writes that one's individual conduct is a result of a combination of social and genetic forces.[464]   One's conduct is learned through education and environment. The awareness of the meaning of one's conduct is learned through specific social ideals. Thus, consciousness of conduct is a consciousness both of the impact of one's education and environment and the social ideals which shape the interpretation of the meaning of one's education and environment.[465]

Within a social context one becomes conscious of one's conduct. By exposure to different tensions within a social context, an individual awakens to

---

[462] Royce, J. The Problem of Christianity, vol I, p. 174.
[463] Ibid., p. 165.
[464] Ibid., p. 127.
[465] Ibid., p. 132.

higher levels of self-consciousness and is able to develop.[466]   This development reflects the Apostle Paul's main thesis that one's moral burden relates not to one's conduct, but to the consciousness of one's conduct. As a result, the power and ability to develop a conscience are a direct result of an individual's nature as a social being.[467]

Both Royce and Schleiermacher argue that the context which develops one's conscience is born of tension. But Royce enlarges this tension to show the way in which the social process exerts various forces which impinge on one another through interpretation. This tension is imparted by the critical judgments which are made concerning the ideals to be cultivated, embodied, and perpetuated by a particular community. These judgments create the dynamics within which the society and the community can develop. In essence, the context of the community is the social matrix for the war between ideals.[468]

In chapter three, Royce's effort to identify a coherent principle which can galvanize contingent realities into a meaningful whole was demonstrated. Through the development of institutions, organizations, traditions and histories, signs are interpreted which create communal ideals.[469]   These interpretations create a communal consciousness.   These interpretations are more than Schleiermacher's advocacy of doctrines and traditions. These interpretations reflect the processes of all communities which must be preserved if the community will endure.

According to Royce, the Pauline Churches are a direct reflection of the way in which Christian religious communal consciousness is formed.[470]   By Paul's interpretation of the Christ-event, signs were interpreted in such a way that a communal consciousness could form around a common, unifying ideal. As such, this interpretation has created a communal consciousness which connects the individual with the ultimate meaning of his or her salvation. This is similar to Schleiermacher's treatment of the influence of Jesus' God-consciousness on all

---

[466] Ibid., p. 136.
[467] Ibid., p. 137.
[468] Ibid., p. 142; 156.
[469] Royce, J. The Problem of Christianity, vol. II, p. 37.
[470] Ibid., p. 38.

believers, but Royce has expanded this notion to suggest it distills the dynamics of all communities.

What is clear from Royce is that the development of individual and communal consciousness takes time. It takes time to develop coherence within an individual personality and it takes time to develop coherence between an individual personality and a communal consciousness.[471] The time-process reflects an intentionality of consciousness in which a coherent, or teleological, orientation can be expressed. The time-process expresses that neither an individual life nor a corporate life are a mere datum of material, but are an interpretation of a vast quantity of material guided in their interpretations by a collection of guiding ideals embedded in custom and tradition.[472] The enduring significance of the community depends on the quality of its participants and the guiding ideals to which the community is committed.

According to Royce, the best expression of the development of communal consciousness and the integration of individuals into these common ideals through the bonds created by interpretation is captured by Paul in I Corinthians 15. Here, Paul articulates, as he interprets, the best explanation for how individuals are joined into one common consciousness through a unifying, all inclusive ideal. In I Corinthians 15, Paul clearly conceives both the diversity of the members and the unity of the body in terms of the 'common hope for the same event.'[473] This common hope for the same event is the unifying event to which all individuals of the community must relate. In relating to this unifying event in a common way individual consciousness is shaped by the common consciousness of the community. Thus, Royce believes the common hope for the resurrection from the dead is the sustaining force in the development of Christian religious consciousness.[474]

In this way, Paul defines the way in which his own religious consciousness has been formed and demonstrates the way in which human solidarity and

---

[471] Ibid., p. 41.
[472] Ibid., p. 43.
[473] Ibid., p. 73.
[474] Ibid., p. 73.

individual destiny are joined in the divine life of the community.[475] This unity and multiplicity is captured within the community and is sustained by the common events, hopes and memories which arouse a common love among all of the community's members. In this way, the common events, hopes, and memories, which reflect a variety of deeds and events, form the individual consciousness through its identification with the communal consciousness.[476]

The Universal Element of Communal Consciousness

Earlier, Royce's criticism of William James for advocating a universal core to individual religious experience was noted. His criticism was leveled not against any universal principle, but against the elevation of an Enlightenment ideal. Royce fundamentally believes that every individual act and experience only gains meaning by being placed in an unifying ideal which originates beyond the individual in the community. As a result, Royce advocated that the idea of salvation and the search for salvation are matters that are restricted to no one type of religion or philosophy, but are interpreted across religions and philosophies as one searches for an unifying ideal.[477] In essence, all religions are social, salvific and teleological. Their universal common core is exemplified by stressing the common experience of the faithful finding the unifying ideal through the interpretation of the multiplicity of manifestations of the contingent religious life.

In chapter five, the legitimation of all true religions as finite expressions of the universal ideal was noted. These expressions, moreover, were various forms and stages on the way to recognition of the religion of loyalty. Since all legitimate religions are concerned with salvation and since the whole world is defined as social, these various manifestations of the religion of loyalty, are expressions of the way in which the individual finds their salvation through the social nature of interpretation. The best expression of this distinction is found in the contrast between Christianity and Buddhism.

---

[475] Ibid., p. 75.
[476] Ibid., p. 81.
[477] Royce, J. Sources of Religious Insight, p. 15.

Royce advocates the supremacy of Christianity and Buddhism over all other common religions on the basis that these two religions best understand and address the universal religious nature of reality. Royce further advocates the supremacy of Christianity over Buddhism because of Christianity's emphasis on the importance of the historical church in which an individual can find the context for an interpretation leading to a salvific ideal. Royce arrives at these conclusions, however, only after drawing elaborate comparisons and contrasts between the two religions. By drawing these comparisons, Royce is able to show both how Christian religious consciousness develops in relation to other religions and how it develops in relation to itself.

Several of the comparisons offered by Royce reflect his belief in the way in which a religion develops and echo suggestions made elsewhere by Schleiermacher. Both Christianity and Buddhism are universal in scope. Both deliberately transcend caste, rank, race and nation by showing how these contingent particulars provide openings to divine insight. Both demonstrate, through missions, their great ability to adapt and assimilate into cultures other than the one in which they originate. Both are redemptive religions, concerned with the salvation of the individual. Each religion preaches purity of heart, kindness towards all, salvation through transformation and the attainment of eternal peace and rest. Both religions appeal to high moral ideals, the example of an historical founder whose life was exemplary, and the production of symbol systems to retain the religious significance of their tradition in order to transmit this tradition to each new generation.[478] As compatible as the two religions appear to be, however, their contrasts are even more striking.

Royce begins by noting that Buddhism, in general, has been considered pessimistic while Christianity, in general, has been considered hopeful. Buddhism emphasizes passionless contemplation, the extinction of individual consciousness and a lack of any kind of sustaining love. Christianity, by contrast, emphasizes active love, the infinite worth of the individual who hopes for personal immortality and the sustaining love of the Father who loves every human eternally.

---

[478] Royce, J. The Problem of Christianity, vol. I, pp. 332-339.

Of more damning significance to Royce is Buddhism's complete lack of emphasis on the development of the community. Because Buddhism never developed a strong sense of community, the ideal of the Beloved Community did not emerge in the collective consciousness of the Buddhist. This failure resulted in the complete inability to show how an individual could be raised into the higher life of the community thereby gaining one's salvation.[479]

Christianity, by contrast, emphasized from the outset that an individual's destiny is the Kingdom of Heaven. Christianity, moreover, symbolized this destiny by emphasizing the importance of the religious community as the church. In this emphasis on the individual finding his or her destiny within the community, Christianity captured the essence of human salvation through the interpretation of the way in which the natural self finds its salvation by being bonded with the social self. Christianity's unique emphasis in its understanding of community is that love, as the spirit of Christianity, unites many individuals in the common bond of the Beloved Community through interpretation. This common bond of love, of 'Pauline charity,' is what Christianity ultimately offers in opposition to Nirvana.[480]

Royce contrasts Christianity with Buddhism and exalts Christianity over Buddhism because Christianity provides the most comprehensive interpretation of the way in which finite signs can be interpreted in order to mediate ultimate reality.[481] Paul discovered this truth through his experience in the social and religious life of the first Christian communities. Through these communities, new institutions, customs, and traditions formed as a result of the interpretations which mediated between finite experiences and the ultimate, unifying ideal. Through Royce, a recognition of the way in which finite particulars mediate infinite ideals is demonstrated.

The development of Christian religious consciousness resulted in the unique identification Christianity gave to an individual's experience of detachment from any unifying ideal and the individual's need for reattachment

[479] Ibid., pp. 339-347.
[480] Ibid., p. 190.
[481] Ibid., p. XVIII.

mediated by the interpretive role of the community. Christianity both identified this need and emphasized an individual's inability to meet this need on his or her own. As a result, Christianity provided the interpretive key for the way in which one could, through interpretation, construct a meaningful ideal which produced understanding for a vast array of individual contingent forces.[482]

Christian religious consciousness develops through identification with the most permanent and indispensable features of Christianity. According to Royce, Christianity has two distinct characteristics which shape religious consciousness. First, Christian religious consciousness emphasizes the recorded teachings and example of an individual person, Jesus Christ, who expressed a certain spirit and expressed this spirit as the way of salvation for all humans. Second, Christianity has never been merely an imitation of the life of Jesus, but an interpretation of the meaning of this life and of the religion started in light of this life.[483] Thus, Christianity is both a religion taught by Jesus to his disciples and a religion which has consisted in the interpretation which later generations have given to the mission and teachings of Jesus.

Thus, the most indispensable and permanent features of Christianity, originally taught by Jesus and subsequently interpreted by later generations, are the need for salvation of the individual, the inescapable moral burden of the individual (expressed in both a natural inheritance as original sin and an awareness of personal guilt), and individual atonement realized through union with the spiritual community.[484] These teachings form the triad of thought which produces the shape of Christian religious consciousness. It is also, according to Royce, the fundamental nature of reality.

The difficulty for Royce is in determining if Jesus and his teachings should hold equal or unequal weight in relation to subsequent interpretation of his life and work. Royce concludes that the life and teaching of Jesus, from the start, were an interpretation and, therefore, the Biblical example itself establishes the primacy of interpretation which takes the contingent forces present in Jesus'

---

[482] Ibid., p. 20.
[483] Ibid., p. 25.
[484] Ibid., p. 35; 41; 43.

historical life and weaves them into a coherent whole which provides meaning. In its interpretation of the life and teachings of Jesus, Christianity interprets religious experience in such a way so as to demonstrate the essence of religion as loyalty and reveal itself as the highest expression of the religion of loyalty. But it is not the only expression.

As Royce established earlier, every legitimate religious interpretation is an expression of the religion of loyalty. In fact, to establish legitimacy as a religion, the interpretation offered by a specific religion must embody essential features of the religion of loyalty. What distinguishes Christianity from all other religious expressions of loyalty, however, is the comprehensive nature of its interpretations. Specifically, Christianity has emphasized both the universality of the ideal community to which one is loyal and the depth and intensity of love expressed and experienced within the context of this community.[485]

Christianity, as a religion, has further emphasized the production and perpetuation of traditions, doctrines and customs which have helped identify its ideal community with the being of God.[486] Clearly, other religions have been inspired by loyalty and other religions have identified their community with God,[487] but Christianity alone has been distinguished by the effort and intensity it has expressed in pursuing an ideal of the visible community built on the invisible spiritual unity present within the church.[488] This spirit, which Royce identifies as the Christian spirit, is found wherever two or three are gathered together by a common ideal which evokes their loyalty to a community created by their interpretation. This particular expression of loyalty, moreover, should express the universal ideal of loyalty which creates unity among all who are loyal everywhere.[489]

Finally, Royce extends Schleiermacher's thoughts on community to demonstrate the way in which the Christian religious consciousness identifies an

---

[485] Ibid., p. 193.

[486] Ibid., p. 195.

[487] See Durkheim, Emile. Elementary Forms of the Religious Life, Translated by Joseph Ward Swain, New York: The Free Press, 1915., for an extensive discussion of the way in which the community has been equated with God.

[488] Royce, J. The Problem of Christianity, vol. I, p. 195.

[489] Royce, J. The Problem of Christianity, vol. II, p. 372.

ultimate aim in life which people run the risk of missing. This ultimate aim is expressed within the Christian ideals which are preserved and perpetuated by the Christian community. The individual, moreover, must find these ideals through the interpretive process contextualized in community. Otherwise, the individual, without relation to any community and its ideals, will wonder aimlessly and not realize the ultimate aim of life.[490]

This ultimate aim relies on the development within the individual of a consciousness of his or her need for salvation. The recognition of this need is a result of insight gained regarding the nature of reality as the unity of facts which once appeared as independent entities with no interconnecting ideal. Insight is gained by the development of a coherent view of the unity of truth.[491] The specific nature of religious insight is the interpretation it is able to provide which offers the best explanation for all aspects of contingent reality.

Reality is religious. As Royce and Schleiermacher both argue the true nature of the world is social and communal. Only a religious interpretation adequately understands this as the true nature of reality.[492] What religious insight teaches is that every human has a need that only a religious understanding can meet. Although alternative interpretations of our need and its satisfaction have been offered, none have been sufficient to provide an overarching ideal which can be sustained in order to displace a religious understanding of the way in which our human need for salvation is satisfied in and through community.[493]

If one fails to develop a recognition of his or her need for salvation, then the religious answer to this need will seem irrelevant. Both the recognition of one's need and the source of its satisfaction through interpretation are inextricably linked. One cannot have knowledge of one without having knowledge of the other.

This lack of knowledge, however, does not dismiss the relevancy or accuracy of this interpretation of reality. This lack of knowledge is an expression of one's lack of development. Religious consciousness is developmental as both

---

[490] Ibid., p. 346; 350; Also, Sources of Religious Insight, p. 12.
[491] Royce, J. Sources of Religious Insight, p. 6.
[492] Ibid., pp. 8-14.
[493] Ibid., p. 17.

Schleiermacher and Royce note. But Royce expands the developmental nature of religion to encompass all of life. Religious consciousness emerges over time as various kinds of religion and in various degrees. The individual experience of both a supreme goal of life and the possibility of missing this supreme goal is the beginning of religious consciousness.[494] The development of religious consciousness results in the dawning awareness of one's need for a community in which all of these signs can gain significance through interpretation.

The emergence of this awareness, moreover, is part of our human consciousness. It develops over time. Its development is inevitable. Unless one's natural development is restricted or retarded, the development of religious consciousness culminates in one's awareness of the need for salvation and the source for satisfying this need. This awareness is universal in its scope and particular in its embodiment. Christian religious consciousness develops because in it is found the true nature and ground of reality.

Royce extends this argument by noting that the human is free and illustrates this in his discussion of the orientation of the will as a will-to-interpret. How one chooses to orient one's will fundamentally determines what meaning one can find for the contingent experiences in life. The community forms the context in which the interpretation of signs so critical for human knowing can occur. As a result, the community forms the foundation in which the processes of communication and cooperation are made possible. Through communication and cooperation one is integrated into the community through the felt unities which mediate one's salvation.[495]

The Role of the Will

Earlier, in chapter five, Royce distinguished the role of the will in his thought by noting the influence of Schopenhauer, but with an important change. In Schopenhauer's thought, the two main activities of the will were the will-to-power and the will-to-resignation. Both expressions of the will embodied the

---

[494] Ibid., p. 12; 19.
[495] Oppenheimer, Frank. op. cit., p. 354.

motivation behind significant human activity. But neither expression fully captured any unifying ideal which could provide a comprehensive expression to guide one's life.

As a result, Royce advocated a third activity of the will, namely, the will-to-loyalty which formed human community. Through the will-to-loyalty, communities could form which nurtured and sustained individual selves. Because of loyalty, communities could be built with enduring customs and traditions. Through the exercise of loyalty, individual selves could unite in community, discover the true aim of life and achieve the fulfillment of this true aim.[496]

Royce advocates the central role of the will-to-loyalty because of its ability to unify the self with its conflicting plans and intentions.[497] Loyalty preserves moral autonomy while providing the ethical context in which moral purpose can be expressed. Therefore, loyalty generates community through willful intention.[498]

Through the will, reason expresses human intention.[499] Reason operates to unify the disparate elements of our life by directing the will in the expression of loyalty.[500] The place of reason, according to Royce's scheme, is similar to Kant. Royce, in fact, sees himself as the logical interpreter of Kant as he translates and transforms Kant's theory of knowledge in order to render the role of the rational will intelligible.[501]

The will, guided by reason, helps the individual perceive the overarching perspective of life. Reason directs the will in the apprehension of an interpretation which provides life with an orienting ideal. Reason works with will to gain insight uniquely religious. Reason directing will helps the individual identify with an all-embracing perspective which constitutes a unified theory of

---

[496] Royce, J. The Problem of Christianity, vol. II, pp. 311-312.
[497] Skrupskelis, Ignas K, "Royce and the Justification of Authority," Southern Journal of Philosophy, 8, pp. 165-170, Summer-Fall, 1970, p. 165.
[498] Ibid., p. 169.
[499] Royce, J. Sources of Religious Insight, p. 120.
[500] Freud argues against this perspective suggesting instead that reason is really the hand-maiden of passion. See, Freud, Sigmund. The Future of an Illusion. New York: Norton, 1961; original German, 1927.
[501] Royce, J. Sources of Religious Insight, p. 123.

knowledge and experience.[502]

The exercise of individual will guides the person in a course of conduct. An attitude or opinion directs the will in the fulfillment of duties, the modification of conduct, and the pursuit of a life dream.[503] Such exercise leads the individual to see that actions and intentions are governed by the reciprocal relation between the will expressed through reason's discernment of personal options and the exercise of the will in submitting itself to the intentions of the community. Thus, no action, intention or understanding of truth is possible unless reason unifies will in the pursuit of an unifying ideal.[504]

Without an unifying ideal, individual experiences not only fail to have meaning, but existence itself fails to make sense. This unifying ideal is proved worthy of our willful allegiance by the prominence of its past history in meeting human needs and the power of its present ability to interpret contingent experiences in a way which provides salvation.[505] The persuasive power of the unifying ideal is its ability to provide a synthesizing view of human deeds and experience. Every interpreted deed is irrevocable. These interpreted deeds are an expression of the individual will-to-interpret. When one expresses one's will through a deed it is performed before a backdrop which interprets the meaning of this deed in relation to the ideal one has embraced for one's life.[506]

Truth and reality establish the validity of this idea. Truth is the expression of ideals and opinions which give rise to deeds which fulfill these ideals. Reality is the expression through deeds of the truth of one's ideals and opinions. Thus, truth and reality, as defined by Royce, are an expression of the adequacy of certain particular deeds which reflect the fulfillment found by the identity with an all-encompassing universal ideal.[507]

Ideals and opinions adjust in accordance with one's experience of their validity. These adjustments reflect an awareness of one's fundamental need of

---

[502] Ibid., p. 137.
[503] Ibid., p. 140.
[504] Ibid., p. 144.
[505] Ibid., p. 151.
[506] Ibid., p. 156.
[507] Ibid., pp. 158-160.

salvation and the way in which one pursues the fulfillment of these fundamental needs in a way which makes sense. Thus, they must become plausible. Deeds are the experiential expression of the multiplicity and contingency of individual life. Ideals are the spiritual expression of the uniformity and coherence one needs in order to find the eternal meaning of life. Together, through interpretation, deeds and ideals express the way in which the contingencies of life are gathered into coherent meaning through the interpretive role of the religious community.[508]

The Moral Burden Which Awakens Human Consciousness

In chapter six, Schleiermacher demonstrated the necessary unity between the religious and the sensible self-consciousness. If the two are not connected, Schleiermacher argued, than there is no avenue by which finite particulars can mediate universal ideals. Royce extends this demonstration by arguing that human consciousness awakens to a higher level of reality when it confronts the great moral burden which every individual must bear.[509] For Royce, awakening to one's moral burden is the starting point for the development of the religious consciousness in all of its manifestations, Christian and otherwise.[510] But the Christian understanding of the moral burden of every individual recognizes and addresses this reality most powerfully.

In contrast to Schleiermacher, who argues the Christian interpretation of life is only pertinent within the Christian community, Royce demonstrates that the Christian doctrine of life best expresses the needs humans have and the manner in which one can work to meet these needs most effectively.[511] The consciousness of one's violation of a standard creates empirical contact with the universal idea of original sin. The idea of original sin articulates the consciousness that every finite individual is influenced by the universal reality of a moral standard which has been violated.[512] The violation of this moral standard is a result of the will

---

[508] Ibid., p. 160.
[509] Royce, J. The Problem of Christianity, vol. I, p. 109.
[510] Ibid., pp. 121-122.
[511] Ibid., p. 112.
[512] Ibid., p. 122.

inclining reason to operate in violation of the established standard.[513]

In Royce's specific treatment of the Christian understanding of the moral burden he emphasizes Paul's teaching from Romans 7. Here, Paul identifies three aspects of sin which are fundamental. First, sin is basic to our nature. Second, sin increases unless checked by divine intervention. And third, sin is both individual and cumulative.[514] All three characteristics highlight the relation the individual has to the community through the interpretation of their life experiences. Since humans are fundamentally social creatures it is inevitable that consciousness develops to a level where one recognizes the reality of these three characteristics.[515]

Royce further identifies sin as the voluntary consent of the individual to violate a reasonable standard one has embraced willingly.[516] Deeds reflect dispositions. Therefore, external deeds which are good reflect a good internal disposition while external deeds which are evil reflect an internal disposition which is evil.[517] Royce is trying to show that concrete reality and historical reality are joined by the bonds of interpretation in which the individual attempts to make sense of all aspects of their lived reality. Ultimately, sin is whatever threatens to destroy the Beloved Kingdom or the love of God and other humans.

The consequence of sin is to miss the desired aim and goal of life. Since sin is universal and the sinner is unable to win personal forgiveness, the universal consequence of unforgiven sin is permanent estrangement from the community which saves.[518] Because the community is that which saves, sins against the community are particularly pernicious.

The most severe sin against the community is the act of disloyalty or betrayal. If one can understand the nature of loyalty then one's consciousness has developed to the level that you can understand the nature of disloyalty.[519] The sin of betrayal is the deliberate violation of the known standard one has

---

[513] Ibid. p. 157.
[514] Ibid., p. 148.
[515] Ibid., p. 176.
[516] Ibid., p. 219.
[517] Ibid., p. 227.
[518] Ibid., pp. 235-236.
[519] Ibid., p. 254.

embraced.[520]   Betrayal breaks ties and ruins unity. It destroys community. Left unredeemed it irreparably damages the spirit of community.

To commit the sin of betrayal, moreover, is to commit an irrevocable deed that fundamentally wounds the integrity of the community. Such an act is not removed by oneself.[521]   Thus, to redeem an act of betrayal, a source outside of oneself must act to bring meaning to the act and integrate the individual back into the life of the community. Otherwise, the destruction of the community in an act of betrayal will inevitably lead to the destruction of the individual. One's actions always impact both an individual and a social self. This reality is inescapable. Therefore, acts of betrayal must be redeemed through the interpretation of these disloyal deeds back into the meaning-making ideal of the loyal community.[522]

The Nature of Salvation

When one's religious consciousness develops to the level in which one recognizes the reality of one's own sin, then the individual has also developed to the level in which he or she recognizes the possibility of obtaining salvation. Salvation is the getting rid of sin and recovering a life of love typified by the spirit of Jesus.[523]

Salvation is the experience of the divine power or principle which saves.[524] Knowledge of this experience of the divine is not simply knowledge mediated through revelation. Knowledge and experience are predicated on the development of religious consciousness to the point where one is aware both of one's need of salvation and the way in which salvation is mediated to the individual. This is the religious paradox: that one must develop an awareness of one's need of salvation before the way in which this salvation can be gained is realized.

This concern with the awareness of one's need for salvation and religion's provision for this need is the essence of all higher religions.   Christianity

---

[520] Ibid., p. 262.
[521] Ibid., p. 265.
[522] Ibid., p. 294.
[523] Ibid., p. 223.
[524] Royce, J. Sources of Religious Insight, p. 25.

158

specifically, and higher religions generally, provide insight into the way of salvation.[525]   The way of salvation is the result of links created between an individual and a community through interpretation.[526]

One of the great obstacles in accepting a religious answer to the individual need of salvation is the problem of evil. Evil results from the actions of nature and humans. Evil, at the hands of humans, is often the most difficult reality to reconcile with one's understanding of the role of the community in mediating one's salvation.[527]   In order to offer a valid theory of salvation, moreover, the religious purpose of evil must be identified. Royce returns to his theory of loyalty to explain the purpose of evil. In fact, all types of evil provide the greatest opportunities to express loyalty.[528]   One is able to redeem evil when one places the meaning of this evil in the broader context of the community.

In essence, evil teaches the spiritual nature of the universe. Without the presence of evil, the identification of good would be impossible.[529]   Evil means different things in different contexts. The religious tradition, moreover, plays a key role in one's perception of evil.   The interpretation given to a specific experience, by a particular community, will determine whether or not it is determined to be evil.[530]

The specific experience of events interpreted as evil provide the context within which character can develop. By overcoming evil one overcomes the greatest obstacle to a religious interpretation of reality. Salvation wages constant war with evil. The two are pitched in a battle for the ultimate explanation of reality as we know it. Salvation is a process which is endless. Salvation is mediated through an interpretation of the past and the future through interpretive acts in the present. These interpretive acts exist only in the context of community

---

[525] Ibid., p. 8; 25.
[526] Ibid., p. 73.
[527] Ibid., p. 219.
[528] Ibid., p. 234.
[529] John Bowker in, Problems of Suffering in Religions of the World, (Cambridge, Eng: Cambridge University Press, 1970) makes a strong case that major religions treat evil and suffering quite differently.   This definition is built on Royce's logic, concerning how we discern truth from error.
[530] Royce, J. Source of Religious Insight, pp. 249-252.

and create the bonds which can conquer the enervating powers of evil.[531]

The community saves. The spirit, which brings salvation, is the redeeming divine spirit that dwells in the church.[532] The spirit, which helps the individual caught in a treasonous act to be restored to the community, exists only in a community and is only expressed through an heroic individual who reconciles those who have betrayed the community back into the community.[533]

In the salvation of a treasonous individual the community expresses the greatest spirit of atonement. Atonement is the turning of the evil of betrayal into good.[534] Royce amplifies this point by using the incident of Joseph and his brothers from the book of Genesis. Here, Joseph experiences the worst betrayal at the hands of his brothers. This misfortune, however, is redeemed for good through Joseph's heroic act of forgiving his brothers and relieving their own physical calamity.[535]

Atonement, by definition, must bring good out of evil.[536] Atonement expresses the divine grace of the community. Since humans are social animals, and since betrayal is the grossest violation of our nature as social animals, atonement and grace redeem traitorous deeds for good in the restoration of an individual to the community which saves.

Communities of atonement are started by unusual individuals in human history. These individuals galvanize others into communities through interpretation of contingent particulars which can mediate the spirit of love and loyalty through the community. These interpretive acts, moreover, create the bonds upon which unity is built and individuals are transformed.[537]

The Early Church is the archetypal example of this type of community. Through the Early Church, many were won over to this spirit of loyalty and experienced atonement. This experience, moreover, gave rise to the expression of the ideal of the 'Beloved Community' which could provide universal salvation for

---

[531] Ibid., p. 377.
[532] Royce, J. The Problem of Christianity, vol. II, p. 363.
[533] Royce, J. The Problem of Christianity, vol. I, p. 377.
[534] Ibid., pp. 366-371.
[535] Ibid., p. 371.
[536] Ibid., p. 373.
[537] Ibid., p. 376.

all humanity.

The community does not simply save in the sense of providing forgiveness. The community saves by helping individuals come to grips with the interpretive ties which exist between an individual and the community. This restoration allows the individual to come to a higher consciousness of the true nature of his or her life and see it in relationship to others within the community. The danger the individual faces is to assume that the individual is the source of his or her own salvation. Instead, the community helps to turn an individual away from a preoccupation with his or her own ability to save him or herself in order to realize that it is only within the community that one finds the true source of salvation.

The central problem of atonement is the restoration of the individual who has betrayed the community. It is only through a voluntary act of the will-to-be-loyal that an individual returns to the community in which saving grace can be found.[538] The act of restoration makes the world better than it would have been if the original act of betrayal had never occurred because the broader concern of discovering universal loyalty has occurred. Thus, the restoration of the traitor's life back into the community changes the tragedy into a triumph.[539]

According to Royce, the atonement of Christ, as the archetype of universal atonement, is not moral reconciliation or penal atonement. It (Christ's atonement) represents the community's exercise through interpretation of its collective will. Thus, the interpretation of Christ's atoning sacrifice is the foundation for establishing the redemptive role of the community in restoring through interpretation every individual alienated from the community. Even if the interpretation of Christ's atoning sacrifice had not occurred within Christianity, human consciousness would have produced an idea like this in order to make sense of the contingent particulars through a coherent, unified whole thereby demonstrating the reality of universal atonement mediated by the community.

---

[538] Ibid., p. 307.
[539] Ibid., pp. 307-308.

Integrative Insights of Schleiermacher and Royce

Thus, the religious community plays an indispensable role in shaping religious consciousness. Both Schleiermacher and Royce have offered unique understandings of the nature of interpretation, of individual religious experience, of religion, of community, of what draws an individual into religious community, and of the interpretive role of the religious community. By integrating Schleiermacher and Royce, a compelling explanation has been offered for how the religious consciousness of an individual is formed. It allows an individual to understand his or her contingent religious experiences by contextualizing these experiences within a coherent center of meaning through the interpretive process of the religious community.

Contingency, as noted, captures the individual's experiences of variety and disharmony which one encounters in daily life. This variable element, comprised of the historical, sociological, economic and psychological situations which the individual faces in his or her historical existence, must be unified if life is to have meaning. Coherence, by contrast, reflects the way in which the religious community transmits a stable, constant ideal within which individuals find meaning for these contingent experiences. This coherent framework is held together by a network of symbolic relations based on a common core of doctrine and tradition and transmits meaning by becoming the source of 'felt unities' between this world and the realm where the ultimate ideal of our lives can be found.

Together, Schleiermacher and Royce have demonstrated that all religious experience is interpreted experience if it is to have meaning. As such, they have also noted that it is impossible to interpret religious experience without such experiences being contextualized within the religious community. In order for an interpretation of religious experience to be considered valid, moreover, it must remain plausible by demonstrating that it continues to offer the best explanation or overriding ideal for the contingent experiences one has throughout their personal life.

Religious communities both shape religious consciousness and are shaped by the individuals who interpret their religious experiences within the context of particular religious communities. As the context in which the interpretation of religious experience occurs, the religious community uses words in particular ways to distill meanings.

Like Wittgenstein, an integration of Schleiermacher and Royce demonstrates how words have meaning by their use in a particular context of real life. Thus, the way in which a particular religious community utilizes language, doctrine, rituals and traditions provides a particular form of community which can serve as a bridge between individuals and ultimate ideals.[540] Through the reciprocal relationship of doctrine and teaching regulating ritual and language use, one is able to realize that individuals do not construct their own meanings or interpretations, but embrace unifying ideals which bring coherence to their random experiences.

Rituals, theological teachings, doctrines and language-use all act as bridges both stimulating new interpretations as they distill traditional insights. Thus, the rituals one practices within the context of community reflect a particular religious interpretation of reality.

The teachings which accompany these rituals convey the theological heritage of the particular religious community. Teachings convey significance. They elevate and diminish different understandings of religious experience gleaned throughout the history of the community. They shape the community's perception of reality. They are indispensable to constructing, transmitting and safeguarding the way in which a particular religious community understands its grand unifying ideal to work.

The doctrines of the community, moreover, are a distillation of the religious use of language, the ritual practices, the teachings of the church, and the experiences of the faithful. These, too, are bridges that form bonds between the individual and the unifying ideal. They both exhibit the essence of individual religious experiences set forth in speech and the way in which ritual participation

---

[540] Wittgenstein, Ludwig. Philosophical Investigations (Oxford: Blackwell, 1968), pp. 31-32.

and communal teaching provide the language forms within which interpretation of these experiences can occur.

The use of religious language, or the religious use of language, is fundamentally tied to the religious context. Both Schleiermacher and Royce recognize this phenomenon. They agree that language use must be contextualized within the religious community to have meaning. As a result, they reveal humanity's nature as a historical-bound reality that, nevertheless, can mediate human transformation.

By contextualizing the religious use of language in a particular religious community, Schleiermacher and Royce have demonstrated the way in which religious communities establish the context in which subjective experiences can make sense. Because the interpretation of religious experience occur within religious communities, it will also be shown that the differences within and among religious communities can explain why people not only report different interpretations of religious experience, but actually have different experiences. That is, different religions provide different unifying ideals to explain the contingent experiences of their adherents.

By utilizing Schleiermacher and Royce, a center of value beyond the self is established. Whether it be full-bodied God-consciousness or the Beloved Community, a realm in which a broader overview of life then is normally perceived is established. If left on their own, moreover, individuals will not only miss this realm, but be entirely incapable of finding any other resources to sustain themselves.

What Schleiermacher and Royce have demonstrated, in opposition to Kant and James, is the role the religious community can play in providing the context within which humanity's particular experiences and society's ultimate ideals can unify through interpretation. Because individuals are not self-sufficient, they cannot gain a sufficient perspective on the world to sustain themselves. Since an individual's resources are inadequate, moreover, they must draw on resources from the communities of which they are a part.

In other words, the model of the interpretive role of the religious community providing a bond between an individual's particular experiences and their need for an ideal in which these experiences can make sense becomes normative for all of life. It is within these communities that sense is made not only of one's own personal experience, but also of the whole experience of the entire community.

Every aspect of experience has the potential to awaken one to the need for an interpretive ideal beyond one's experience. Every encounter with the shared history of the religious community (rituals, doctrines, traditions), moreover, can also awaken the individual's need for an interpretive ideal beyond particular experiences. Together, these elementary and complex social experiences bridge the gap between historical existence and the place where the ultimate ideal which makes sense of the individual's historical existence resides.

The biggest obstacle both men identify is the fact these historically-bound realities, which are meant to mediate between the individual and their salvation, can become the focus of salvation itself. That is, rituals are no longer used to usher one beyond the particularity of one's experience. The experience itself is all that has meaning. But this, as Royce and Schleiermacher note, fails to recognize that unless one sees the ritual as having interpretive meaning beyond itself, no bond can emerge which ties one's individual life together with a sustaining ideal.

This does not mean communities should suppress individual expression or personal freedom. It simply means that meaning is found within the community. The community provides structure for the contingent self. It orients the individual in his or her interface with the world. It reflects the way in which life is seen as all of one piece. It is within the religious community that one learns how to look beyond the resources of oneself to find meaning.

Throughout this project, the inadequacy of the Enlightenment ideal of the unencumbered self, freely choosing, prior to all social and historical determinations has been demonstrated. The interpretive role of the religious community in Schleiermacher and Royce makes clear that the individual self is fundamentally wedded to the community of which he or she is a part. By contextualizing the individual within the community we have subsequently tried to show how the process of interpretation establishes the bonds which mediate eternal meaning to the temporal experiences of one's contingent human life.

At the beginning of Section II, an illustration from Robert Bellah was offered to indicate the way in which competing ideals, equality and individualism, often co-exist in the same community. The illustration suggests that no community ever has a settled understanding of its overall ideal. Ideals compete for prominence as the best explanatory hypothesis for contingent experience. Communities embed these ideals and the structures of communities mediate these ideals to their members.

Both Schleiermacher and Royce recognize this fact. They take issue not with the problem of competing ideals, but with the inadequacy of the Enlightenment ideal to provide any ultimate, unifying meaning. Both men recognize that humans are not only social animals by nature, but this social nature only makes sense when placed in the broader context of the communal ideal. In seeking for the best overall communal ideal which explained the reality they faced, Schleiermacher and Royce both identified the way in which particular cultures, as communities, embody ultimate ideals which provide meaning.

That is to say, both believed certain overarching ideals were universal, but every ideal was mediated by particular communities. The question they addressed concerned not the relativity of all ideals, but how does the human form bonds with ultimate ideals that bring meaning to their life? Humans have unique needs that only religion addresses. They become aware of these needs through unique experiences which only religion explains. What explanatory hypothesis, or overarching ideal, provides the best explanation for the reason humanity has these needs and the meaning which unifies their experiences?

Only within the religious community, as both a mediating link to the eternal ideal and the locus of all necessary elements for the interpretive process, can one find the need-satisfying explanation for the multiplicity of one's experiences. Laboring against the error of the Enlightenment, Schleiermacher and Royce both recognized that the human is a social, historical, and culturally conditioned being.

The individual, moreover, does not confer meaning and value outside his or her contextualization within society, history, and culture. But does this imply that if the Enlightenment ideal collapses, conferring meaning in religions and morality through reason alone, that there are no universal ideals worthy of one's time or allegiance?

Absolutely not. Both Schleiermacher and Royce anticipated the very problems that the current discussions have identified, but with an important corrective. Whereas the current debate has collapsed into an exclusive preoccupation with all forms of particularity, Schleiermacher and Royce have advocated that it is not the transcendental ego, with its exchange house of the unity of apperception conferring meaning and value, but the community of interpretation which helps make sense of one's experiences in life. That is, both Schleiermacher and Royce direct one's attention to seek for a grand unifying ideal which can elevate humanity.

Nevertheless, one cannot get to this ideal without help and without being true to one's nature. Therefore, one must neither set aside our history, society, and culture, nor look to it alone for the provision of ultimate meaning in life. History, society, and culture, and all the artifacts which comprise history, society, and culture are all signs which, when interpreted, elevate the individual to a spiritual realm.

Thus, Schleiermacher and Royce help one see that the community is not the barrier to fulfillment, but the only place where the resources to discover fulfillment can be found. Within every culture and community reside enough artifacts that, when interpreted as signs, can lead one into a realm where one can find a unifying life ideal. The problem is individuals seldom look beyond their temporal, historical contingency and spend much of their conscious time focused only on the contingency itself. Unfortunately, there is no ultimate meaning found if one simply adds up one's contingent experiences. They must be united to have meaning.

Thus, when one considers the rituals, traditions, doctrines and uses of language within a community one must recognize that these are both contingent to particular communities and capable of elevating one to the eternal ideal. All of these elements work in their own way to structure community, to express one's need for an ultimate ideal, to confer the grace that only comes when one connects with these ideals through interpretation.

The process of interpretation is the process of building bonds between one's eternal ideals and one's historical contingencies. It is the individual, existing within the mediating process of interpretation anchored to community, that allows the individual to grasp or gain contact with a realm which is beyond him or herself; a realm where one's ultimate need to have life make sense is satisfied.

Thus, communities establish access to ultimate ideals through interpretation. By providing the context in which humans connect with ultimate ideals, communities also generate the ideals worth pursuing. One's experiences within community are not ultimate, but they are signs of ultimacy if one can find the interpretive key which unifies them.

Thus, when one reads criticisms of Royce for his failure to attend adequately to the historicity of Jesus, for example, this should not be troublesome. Royce is concerned about something much deeper. He is concerned about the loss of contact with ultimate ideals and the loss of interest in finding any ultimate meaning in life. If all of an individual's experiences are contingent and no single experience leads to contact with a realm of ultimate ideals, then that person is the most miserable of creatures.

Historical contingencies must provide bridges to the ultimate ideals which unify life. Interpretation in community builds these bridges and establishes the bonds between one's personal life and one's ultimate destiny. Thus, one is always both acting and interpreting these actions. This poses no problem for either Schleiermacher or Royce. What is problematic is how one acts and interprets in relation to an ultimate ideal. Individual lives must have meaning beyond their contingent experiences in a pluralistic universe. But contingent experiences do matter as the links between one's personal life and the ultimate ideal which confers meaning.

Because of the interpretive role of the religious community, Schleiermacher and Royce are able to demonstrate that personal experiences matter because they connect individuals through communities, thus they connect with ultimate ideals. Since individuals are contingent persons it can be no other way. Meaning must be found through one's history. And Schleiermacher and

Royce help find this meaning.

Schleiermacher and Royce do not satisfy all of our questions. What Schleiermacher and Royce point to is not a proof of the way life is, but an interpretation of how ultimate meaning can be found in life. By pursuing ultimate ideals through the mediating role of the community one can find meaning for one's contingent, historically-bound life through a unifying ideal which matters.

Chapter Eight

Concluding Thoughts

Several ideas have been established throughout this dissertation. First, the interpretive process is not an oscillation between twin foci, as in the hermeneutical circle. Rather, by expanding the hermeneutical circle through the triadic process of Josiah Royce, the hermeneutical circle can become an ascending spiral. As an ascending spiral, greater clarity is gained as one places the contingent experience of one's individual life into an overarching ideal which provides meaning. In essence, the most sufficient explanation of the particulars will be the most sustainable ideal.

Next, it has been demonstrated that the use of language is a bridge building, bond forming activity. Language-use is confined to context. Within its appropriate contexts, language-use conveys particular meanings. As such, language itself becomes a bridge in which a bond can form between contingent experiences and a coherent unifying ideal.

Then, it has been demonstrated that it is within communities, which contextualize language use, that interpretation can occur. Interpretation is the meaning-making process. It is the spiritual dynamic which elevates an individual above his or her self-creating, self-sustaining Enlightenment ideal in order to recognize that a more plausible explanation for individual experiences exists.

In addition, it has been demonstrated that every historical, contingent reality is a sign which must be interpreted if it is to have meaning. In other words, individual historical existence, on its own, does not make sense. An individual does not have within his or her own historical existence the resources to manufacture an overarching and unifying ideal. Therefore, if they are to have meaning, historical contingencies must be seen as the particular signs which need interpretation through community.

What is established in chapters four and five is that communities form around shared understandings. Communities both articulate these understandings to others and exist as a sign by which an individual can encounter the realities they embody. As shared understandings they form heavenly bonds, or felt unities, which provide unity to one's life.

Genuine communities differ from common communities by the ideals which they embody. Common communities are formed from race-consciousness or natural features. Genuine communities, by contrast, exist at a higher level of reality as historical embodiments of spiritual ideals. Every member of a genuine community, moreover, exists as a member of a natural community. But every member of a natural community does not necessarily ascend or awaken to the spiritual dimension of genuine communities.

Communities, moreover, reflect the social nature of reality. They are human communities, capable of transmitting connection with a universal ideal. As such, they are signs which establish a bridge between the individual experience and the spiritual reality. By interpretation within the context of community, moreover, an individual is able to connect with the spiritual ideal which unifies life.

Within communities, language is used in a particular way. The religious use of language both reflects and influences the shape of the community's consciousness. Language is a human reality. As a human reality, however, it is able to communicate a spiritual ideal. Therefore, the spiritual ideal that unifies life must be communicated through finite language forms.

Preaching is one example of the religious use of language and reflects the way in which language can be used to build community. Preaching can provide a mediating link between the individual consciousness and the unifying ideal of the communal consciousness.

Culture, doctrine, tradition, and Scripture all influence the formation of community and contribute to the unique historical embodiments of the communal ideal. As such, they mediate particular spiritual realities. The artifacts of culture, doctrine, tradition and Scripture are signs which not only distill the nature of particular communities, but also are interpreted so the individual connects with this unifying ideal.

Because humans exist within a social and historical realm they must find signs within this realm which can transmit spiritual meaning. Two such signs are death and suffering. Frequently, however, the religious quest is side-tracked by unexpected death or undeserved suffering. Both Schleiermacher and Royce recognize in death and suffering not a barrier, but a passageway. Death and suffering, like moral failure and sin, can seem like limitations. They can also be awakenings to new insight. Death and suffering are human realities. They are fundamental to human existence. Therefore, the human must discover meaning in these fundamental realities. When interpreted, death and suffering help create a mediating link between a human's contingent experience of suffering and the spiritual realm in which these experiences mediate meaning.

In a unique way, Schleiermacher and Royce are radical realists with a unique slant. Every contingent reality must be interpreted to be a fact. In addition, every contingent reality can also serve as a sign for interpretation. As such, they depict our understanding of reality as an ascending spiral in which greater understanding can be gained by discovering an overarching ultimate ideal which can provide meaning.

As a particular, but important illustration of this point, consider the example of Jesus. As a historical person, he is a finite particular. As interpreted by the Early Church, he is the sign which leads to the discovery of the ultimate, unifying ideal. Thus, his contingent life, on its own, is a variety of teachings and experiences which lack a coherent center. By recognizing the strength of his God-consciousness or the way in which this God-consciousness was interpreted in the Early Church, Jesus, the historical person, becomes the resurrected sign producing contact with the transcendent realm which saves.

Interpretation and community are inextricably linked. Communities form by the bonds created by interpretation. As a result, interpretation within the community is the bond-building, felt-unity producing activity which leads to contact with the universal ideal that saves.

It is now clear that the religious community establishes the context in which interpretation can occur. Interpretation within community establishes the unifying bonds which join an individual to ultimate ideals in a way which mediates salvation. These interpretation-formed bonds endure until they no longer make sense. When their plausibility breaks down then a new interpretation must be given which provides the best explanation, or overarching ideal, within which one's contingent realities can be given meaning.

Out of these interpretations, communal consciousnesses are formed. The community, as the repository of these consciousnesses, fundamentally shapes the signs of historical contingency which interpretation uses to produce its meaning-making ideal. These communities also become a sign themselves; a complex sign in which one can experience the mediation of salvation through contact with the community.

Interpretation, within the context of community, is the way in which the unifying ideal can make sense of the lived particulars. Because Christianity makes the most sense through its interpretation of these contingent factors it is to be given precedence over all other religious interpretations of reality including Buddhism. As such, in offering its interpretation of particular signs, Christianity generates new signs which, in turn, must be interpreted.

Signs are given to be interpreted. The interpretation of signs is contextualized within community. Signs, therefore, are contingent realities contextualized in community. When they are interpreted then they are given meaning. This process of interpreting signs within the context of community is the way in which salvation is mediated. Preaching, Scripture, Baptism and the Lord's Supper are all signs which, when interpreted, convey deeper meaning.

Prayer and the will-to-interpret are internal orientations which reflect an intentionality of consciousness. Through prayer and the will-to-interpret, internal motivations are revealed which make it possible for interpretation to provide meaning. Both prayer and the will-to-interpret are spiritual activities which influence the way one searches for the all-encompassing unifying ideal which elevates natural consciousness into a spiritual realm in which all of life can make sense.

For Schleiermacher, the unifying ideal is to discover within one's individual God-consciousness the fullness of the God-consciousness of Jesus Christ. For Royce, the unifying ideal is the spirit of loyalty in which every contingent reality can be interpreted in a way that provides ultimate meaning. For both, the bonds formed by interpretation join an individual to a community in which the source of his or her salvation can be realized; a realm in which one finds the all encompassing life ideal by which all of life's contingent experiences can be given meaning and make sense.

Postscript: Issues for Further Research

In synthesizing Schleiermacher and Royce an inevitable question arises regarding how such an integration addresses the present and immediate future of discussions regarding the interpretive role of the religious community. Several issues deserving our attention, but lying beyond the scope of this project, come to mind.

Of primary concern is the growing retrenchment of communal life away from genuine and true communities and back into natural and common communities. Both Schleiermacher and Royce recognized that communities form on two primary concerns. Either a community forms as a natural (Royce) and common (Schleiermacher) community based on ethnic, class, gender and other specific and exclusive criteria or genuine (Royce) and true (Schleiermacher) communities form by adherence to an elevating spiritual ideal. Schleiermacher and Royce both believe true and genuine communities are not only the best form of community, but is the only form of community which is aligned with the fundamental nature of reality.

What is happening presently is not only the natural division of modern society along ethnic, gender and class lines, but the angry advocacy of such division. What was originally envisioned as the opportunity to integrate vast arrays of immigrants into a mainstream culture is now being sacrificed on the altar of a self-serving ideal.

Royce, in particular, offers a helpful corrective to this current demise, but it is a corrective few leaders are willing to heed. Royce's ideas of the right use of provincialism and the need for training in loyalty both presupposed integration into the grand unifying ideal of Democracy. Such an ideal called the powerful to willingly sacrifice advantages of power in order to elevate new immigrants into the potentialities of a Democratic community. By identifying the role of families, clubs, sports teams and other forms of provincial loyalty Royce demonstrates the way in which communal loyalty can be cultivated in order to sustain the broader ideal of the Democratic community.

With the collapse of integration into a grand unifying ideal of Democracy and the emergence of hostile advocacy of one's own self-interest, such calls for self-sacrifice are often ridiculed and frequently ignored. This has only exacerbated the attendant problems in American culture. The possibilities inherent in Schleiermacher and Royce provide resources for this contemporary discussion and all of its attendant problems.

A second area for future research and closely related to this first area is an integration of Royce's theory of community with the work of such contemporary social and religious thinkers as Jurgen Habermas, Robert Wuthnow and George Lindbeck. Habermas' attempt to unify action-theory and social-theory through communicative activity illustrates the way in which authentic language use both builds and reflects particular communities as contexts of specific discourse as outlined in Wuthnow's concept of communities of discourse. Both thinkers parallel George Lindbeck's advocacy of a cultural-linguistic approach to religious doctrine as a demonstration of the way in which language use follows specific rules of particular communities. As provocative as these thinkers are, however, many of these ideas are foreshadowed in the integrated work of Schleiermacher and Royce. There is no need to recite these places, but there is a need to demonstrate the way in which several neglected ideas from both Schleiermacher and Royce address many of these current concerns in a provocative manner.

A third area of further research concerns the frightening implications of a declining common symbol base in American thought and culture. As communities continue to erode along natural lines of gender and class, and further assert one's ethnic identity over one's national citizenship, how can the populace hope to recover a common symbol system and language form which can provide a unifying base for national dialogue. And, if such a common base is not restored, is it realistic even to hope for any progress towards fulfillment of the Beloved Community.

A fourth area amplifies this third one and concerns the relationship between the integrating power of particular religions and the growing reality of religious pluralism. Both Schleiermacher and Royce not only assumed an evolutionary and progressive development of the religious community, but believed the Christian religious community was the highest expression of this process. Royce, in particular, expanded beyond this discussion to ponder if a time would come when the increasing de-Christianizing of Western Civilization would lead to the emergence of a common symbol base beyond all particular religions. Neither man could imagine what confronts the world presently. With the renewal of religion generally and the growing retrenchment of Fundamentalism in all of its religious expressions--Christian and otherwise--specifically, the divisive dynamics inherent in ethnic, gender and class divisions is escalating within religious communities. Rather then a progressive upward movement towards realization of the Beloved Community, the religious world now stands in a more divided state than either man could have ever imagined. This does not dismiss or destroy the validity of both Schleiermacher and Royce in advocating such movement, but it does suggest the difficulty the human spirit faces in embracing an evolutionary scheme which takes one beyond the boundaries of their own particular religion.

A supplementary concern is whether or not contemporary research can verify the legitimacy of overcoming self-love and self-interest to develop love and loyalty to an ultimate community. As noted earlier, America has co-existed with the twin ideals of equality and individualism. The unremitting question lingers whether or not individualism can sustain itself or if its emergence has in effect sown the seeds of its own demise in contributing to the erosion of the communal spirit which initially elevated this ideal as a part of its guiding vision and then embedded this ideal through its rituals and festivals of freedom.

A subsequent issue is whether or not the ideals of a community, preserved in and by the traditions, doctrines and customs of that community, can provide plausible explanations for how communities form and subsequently integrate members into their ideals. Ideals like martyrdom, patriotism, and duty need the traditions, rituals and customs of particular communities in order to integrate these ideals into the individuals who constitute these communities.

An inherent danger in Royce is his open optimism about the positive outcomes of ongoing interpretation. For example, in his use of 'the Traveler' who enters new mind sets, he sees this analogy as inevitably progressive and good. To extend this analogy, however, what happens if the currency of the new mind set goes bankrupt before 'the Traveler' can exchange his currency for more reliable currency which will retain its value. Thus, part of the current resurgence of particularity is a direct result of the collapse of the plausibility of the modern mentality. In defense of Royce, however, 'the Traveler' can assert a viable image for how one can proceed when the way seems unclear.

In addition, both Schleiermacher and Royce offer rich resources for the way in which communities, which contextualize language and symbol use, become interpretive communities which convey meaning. In this way, the emergence of discourse as a specific form of language use contextualized within an interpretive community can address many of the relevant concerns raised by such diverse thinkers as Derrida, Saussure, Gadamer and David Tracy.

Finally, Schleiermacher and Royce offer a rich panoply of resources for an integrated view of the religious community which is true of all communities. By demonstrating the way in which religious rituals, religious ideas and religious doctrines all combine with ethical principles within communal institutions to form and reflect the authenticity of human experience, Schleiermacher and Royce identify a dynamic illustrative of the religious nature of all true communities. This integration directs one's attention to the dynamic play of specific forces which build particular communities with the potential not only to integrate individuals into their specific ideals, but also to cultivate the capacity to transcend all forms of human particularity.

178

Selected Bibliography

I. Royce:

General Bibliography

Skrupskelis, Ignas K. The Basic Writings of Josiah Royce. Edited with an Introduction by John J. McDermott. Chicago: The University of Chicago Press, 1969.

Primary Sources

_____Royce, Josiah. Fugitive Essays. Cambridge, MA: Harvard University Press, 1920.

Royce, Josiah. George Fox As a Mystic. Cambridge, MA: Harvard University Press, 1913, detached from Harvard Theological Review, v. 6, 1913.

Royce, Josiah. Race Questions, Provincialism, and Other American Problems. New York: The Macmillan Company, 1908.

Royce, Josiah. Sources of Religious Insight. New York: Octagon Press, 1977; reprint of original published in 1912.

Royce, Josiah. The Hope of the Great Community. New York: Macmillan Company, 1916.

Royce, Josiah. The Letters of Josiah Royce. Edited with an Introduction by John Clendenning. Chicago: The University of Chicago Press, 1970.

Royce, Josiah. The Philosophy of Loyalty. New York: The Macmillan Company, 1908.

Royce, Josiah. The Problem of Christianity, vol. I, II. New York: The Macmillan Company, 1913.

Royce, Josiah. The World and the Individual, vol. I, II. New York: Dover, 1959; originally published in 1902.

Royce, Josiah. William James and Other Essays on the Philosophy of Life. New York: Macmillan Company, 1911.

180

Anthologies

The Basic Writings of Josiah Royce, vol. I, II. Edited with an Introduction by John J. McDermott. Chicago: The University of Chicago Press, 1969.

The Philosophy of Josiah Royce. Edited with an Introduction by John K. Roth. Indianapolis: Hackett Publishing Company, 1982.

Secondary Sources

Philosophy in the Twentieth Century. Edited with an Introduction by William Barrett and Henry D. Aiken. San Francisco: Harper and Row, 1962.

Banks, Robert. Paul's Idea of Community. Grand Rapids, MI: Eerdmans, 1980.

Clendenning, John. The Life and Thought of Josiah Royce. Madison, WI: The University of Wisconsin Press, 1985.

Corrington, Robert S. The Community of Interpreters. Macon, GA: Mercer University Press, 1987.

Cotton, James H. Royce On the Human Self. Cambridge, MA: Harvard University Press, 1954.

Di Pasquale, Ralph. The Social Dimensions of the Philosophy of Josiah Royce. Rome: Pontificio Ateneo Antoniana, 1961.

Fuss, Peter. The Moral Philosophy of Josiah Royce. Cambridge, MA: Harvard University Press, 1965.

Kuklick, Bruce. Josiah Royce: An Intellectual Biography. Indianapolis: Bobbs-Merrill, 1972.

Marcel, Gabriel. Royce's Metaphysics. Translated by Virginia and Gordon Ringer, Chicago: H. Regnery, 1956.

Oppenheim, Frank. Royce's Voyage Down Under. Lexington, KY: University of Kentucky Press, 1980.

Oppenheim, Frank. Royce's Mature Ethics. Notre Dame, IN: University of Notre Dame Press, 1993.

Oppenheim, Frank. Royce's Mature Philosophy of Religion. Notre Dame, IN: University of Notre Dame Press, 1987.

Peirce on Signs: Writings on Semiotic by Charles Sanders Peirce. Edited by James Hoopes. Chapel Hill, NC: The University of North Carolina Press, 1991.

Shapiro, Vivian M. The Philosophy and Social Thought of Josiah Royce. Ann Arbor, MI: University Microfilms, 1967.

Smith, Grover. Josiah Royce's Seminar, 1913-1914: As Recorded in the Notebooks of Harry T. Costello. New Brunswick, NJ: Rutgers University Press, 1963.

_____Smith, John E. Royce's Social Infinite. New York: The Liberal Arts Press, 1950.

Wilson, Raymond. In Quest of Community: Social Philosophy in the United States, 1860-1920.

Articles

_____"Community in Royce: An Interpretation," M. L. Briody, Transactions of the Peirce Society, 5, 221-242, Fall, 1969.

"A Model for a Public Theology," Linnell E. Cady, Harvard Theological Review, 80:193-212, April, 1987.

"Josiah Royce's Philosophy of Loyalty: A Hermeneutical Tool for Pauline Theology," D. W. Dottever, American Journal of Theology and Philosophy, 7, 3, pp. 149-163, Summer, 1986.

"Royce and Khomyakov On Community As Process," W. J. Gavin, Studies in Soviet Theology, 15, pp. 119-128, June, 1975.

"Royce and Kant: Loyalty and Duty," J. Grady, British Social Phenomenology, 6, pp. 186-193, October, 1975.

"A Triangular Perspective of Royce," J. D. Hassett, Thought, 42, pp. 69-83, Spring, 1967.

"Royce and Husserl: Some Parallels and Food for Thought," J. Kegley, Transactions of the Peirce Society, 14, pp. 184-199, Summer, 1978.

"From Consensus to Consent: A Plea for a More Communicative Ethic," George McKenny, Soundings, 1991, 74, 3-4, Fall-Winter, pp. 427-457.

"Josiah Royce and George H. Mead On the Nature of the Self," D. L. Miller, Transactions of the Peirce Society, 11, pp. 67-89, Summer, 1975.

"Josiah Royce: Analyst of Religion as Community," Michael Novak, American Philosophy and the Future, pp. 193-218.

"A Roycean Road to Community," Frank Oppenheim, International Philosophical Quarterly, 10, pp. 341-377, September, 1970.

"The Idea of Spirit in the Mature Royce," Frank Oppenheim, Transactions of the Peirce Society, 19, 4, pp. 381-395, Fall, 1983.

"Royce and the Justification of Authority," Ignas K. Skrupskelis, Southern Journal of Philosophy, 8, pp. 165-170, Summer-Fall, 1970.

"The Value of Community: Dewey and Royce," John E. Smith, Southern Journal of Philosophy, 12, pp. 469-479, Winter, 1974.

"Royce and James on Psychical Research," Beatrice H. Zedler, Transactions of the Peirce Society, 10, pp. 235-252, Fall, 1974.

II. Schleiermacher:

General Bibliography

Tice, Terrence. Schleiermacher Bibliography. Princeton, NJ: Princeton Theological Seminary, 1984.

Collected Works

Saemtliche Werke. Berlin: Reimer, 1840-84.

Primary Sources

_____Schleiermacher, F. D. E. The Christian Faith. Edinburgh: T. and T. Clark, 1989.

Schleiermacher, F. D. E. Brief Outline of Theology as a Field of Study. Translated by Terrence Tice. Lewiston, NY: The Edwin Mellen Press, 1990.

Schleiermacher, F. D. E. The Christian Household. Translated by Dietrich Seidel and Terrence Tice. Lewiston, NY: Edwin Mellen Press, 1991.

Schleiermacher, F. D. E. The Christmas Eve. Translated with an Introduction by Terrence Tice. Richmond, VA: John Knox Press, 1967.

Schleiermacher, F. D. E. Hermeneutics: The Handwritten Manuscripts. Edited by Heinz Kimmerle, Translated by James Duke and Jack Forstman. Missoula, MT: Scholars Press, 1977.

Schleiermacher, F. D. E. Introduction to Christian Ethics. Nashville: Abingdon Press, 1989.

Schleiermacher, F. D. E. Kleine Schriften und Predigten. Berlin: Walter de Guyter, 1969-70.

Schleiermacher, F. D. E. Life of Jesus. Edited with an Introduction by Jack Verheyden. Philadelphia: Fortress Press, 1975.

Schleiermacher, F. D. E. Life of Schleiermacher as Unfolded in his Autobiography and Letters. Translated by Frederica Rowan. London: Smith, Elder and Co., 1860.

Schleiermacher, F. D. E. Luke: A Critical Study. Translated with an Introduction by Terrence N. Tice. Lewiston, NY: Edwin Mellen Press, 1993.

Schleiermacher, F. D. E. On Religion: Speeches to the Cultured Among

Its Despisers. (1799 edition) Translated with an Introduction by Richard Crouter.
New York: Cambridge University Press, 1988.

Schleiermacher, F. D. E. On Religion: Speeches to the Cultured Among
Its Despisers. (1806 edition) Translated by John Oman, Introduced by Rudolf
Otto. San Francisco: Harper and Row, Publishers, Incorporated, 1958.

Schleiermacher, F. D. E. On the Glaubenslehre: Two Letters. Translated
by James Duke and Francis Fiorenza. Chico, CA: Scholars Press, 1981.

Schleiermacher, F. D. E. Selected Sermons. Selected and translated by
Mary F. Wilson. New York: Funk and Wagnalls, 1890.

Schleiermacher, F. D. E. Servant of the Word. Translated with an
Introduction by Dawn De Vries. Philadelphia: Fortress Press, 1987.

Schleiermacher, F. D. E. Soliloquies. Translated by H. Friess. Chicago:
Open Court, 1926.

Schleiermacher, F. D. E. Vaterlandische Predigten: eine Auswahl.
Berlin: Staatspolitischer Verlag, 1919-1920.

Secondary Sources

Barth, Karl. Protestant Theology in the 19th Century. Translated and
reissued. Valley Forge, PA: Judson Press, 1973.

Barth, Karl. The Theology of Schleiermacher. Translated by Geoffrey W.
Bromiley. Grand Rapids, MI: William Eerdmans, 1982.

_____Bauer, Johannes. Schleiermacher als patriotischer Prediger. Giessen: A.
Lopelmann, 1908.

Brandt, Richard. The Philosophy of Schleiermacher. New York:
Greenwood Press, 1968.

Dawson, Jerry. Friedrich Schleiermacher, The Evolution of a Nationalist.
Austin, TX: University of Texas Press, 1968.

Gerrish, Brian A. A Prince of the Church. Philadelphia: Fortress Press,
1984.

_____Hodgson, Peter. The Formation of Historical Theology. New York: Harper and Row, 1966.

_____Klemm, David E. The Hermeneutical Inquiry: I and II. Atlanta, GA: Scholars Press, 1986.

Niebuhr, Richard R. Schleiermacher on Christ and Religion. New York: Charles Scribner's Sons, 1964.

Palmer, Richard E. Hermeneutics: Interpretation Theory in Schleiermacher, Dilthey, Heidegger, and Gadamer. Evanston, ILL: Northwestern University Press, 1969.

Pannenberg, Wolfhart. The Church. Translated by Keith Crim. Philadelphia: Westminster Press, 1983.

Pannenberg, Wolfhart. Ethics. Translated by Keith Crim. Philadelphia: Westminster Press, 1981.

Redeker, Martin. Friedrich Schleiermacher: Life and Thought. Translated by John Wallhausser. Philadelphia: Fortress Press, 1973.

_____Schotte, Watlher von. Friedrich Schleiermacher: Patriotische Predigten. Berlin: R. Hobbing, 1935.

Strauss, David F. The Christ of Faith and the Jesus of History: a Critique of Schleiermacher's 'Life of Jesus.' Translated, edited and with an introduction by Leander Keck. Philadelphia: Fortress Press, 1977.

Thiselton, Anthony C. New Horizons in Hermeneutics. Grand Rapids, MI: Zondervan Publishing House, 1992.

Wyman, Walter E. The Concept of Glaubenslehre: Ernst Troeltsch and the Theological Heritage of Schleiermacher. Chico, CA: Scholars Press, 1983.

Articles

"Hermeneutics Today: Some Skeptical Remarks," Hendrik Birus, New German Critique, 1987, 42, Fall, pp. 71-78.

"Medium is the Message: a Revisionist Reading of Augustine's

Experience of Grace According to Schleiermacher and McLuhan," G. N. Boyd, Anglican Theological Review, 56:189-201, April, 1974.

"Schleiermacher's Test for Truth: Dialogue in the Church," Winfried Cordman, Journal of the Evangelical Theological Society, 26:321-328, Spring, 1983.

"Schleiermacher's Hermeneutic and Its Critics," Richard Corliss, Religious Studies, September, 1993, v. 29, 3:363-384.

"Rhetoric and Substance in Schleiermacher's Revision of The Christian Faith," Richard Crouter, Journal of Religion, 60:285-306, July, 1980.

"Friedrich Schleiermacher and the Separation of Church and State," Jerry F. Dawson, Journal of Church and State, Spring, 1965, 7:214-225.

"The Understanding of Language by F. Schlegel and Schleiermacher," H. J. Forstman, Soundings, Summer, 1968, 51:146-155.

"Das Problem der Sprache in Schleiermacher's Hermeneutik," H. G. Gadamer, Z Theologie Kirche, 65, 4:445-458, 1968.

"F. Schleiermacher's Theory of the Limited Communitarian State," J. Hoover, Canadian Journal of Philosophy, 20:241-260, June, 1990.

"Schleiermacher as a Calvinist: a Comparison of Calvin and Schleiermacher on Providence and Predestination," W. L. Moore, Scottish Journal of Theology, 24:167-183, May, 1971.

"Schleiermacher on Language and Feeling," Richard R. Niebuhr, Theology Today, July, 1960, 17:150-167.

"Immediacy and the Text: Friedrich Schleiermacher's Theory of Style and Interpretation," T. Pfau, Journal of History of Ideas, 51:51-73, Ja-March, 1990.

"Interpretation, Influence and Religion," Wayne Proudfoot, Soundings, 61:378-99, Fall, 1978.

"Schleiermacher's Political Thought and Activity, 1806-1813," R. C. Raack, Church History, December, 1959, 28:374-390.

"Continuity, Christ and Culture: a Study of F. Schleiermacher's Christology," J. S. Reist, Journal of Religious Thought, 26, 3:18-40, 1969.

"The Role of Tradition in Schleiermacher Theology," R. G. Wilburn, Encounter, Summer, 1962, 23:300-315.

"Schleiermacher and Feuerbach on Intentionality of Religious Consciousness," R. Williams <u>Journal of Religion,</u> 53:424-455, October, 1973.

"Hermeneutics and the Critique of Ideology," J. Wolff, <u>Sociological Review,</u> Nov., 1975, 23, 4:811-828.

III. General:

Anderson, Eugene and Pauline. Political Institutions and Social Change in Continental Europe in the Nineteenth Century. Berkeley: University of California Press, 1968.

Bellah, Robert. Beyond Belief. San Francisco: Harper and Row, 1970.

Berger, Peter. The Sacred Canopy. Garden City, NY: Doubleday, 1967.

Bowker, John. Problems of Suffering in Religions of the World. Cambridge, Eng: Cambridge University Press, 1970.

Durkheim, Emile. The Elementary Forms of the Religious Life. New York: The Free Press, 1965; originally printed in the United States in 1915 by George Allen and Unwin Ltd., originally published in France in 1912.

Freud, Sigmund. The Future of an Illusion. New York: Norton Press, 1961; originally published in German in 1927.

Gadamer, Hans Georg. Truth and Method. London: Sheed and Ward, 1975.

Geertz, Clifford. The Interpretation of Cultures. New York: Basic Books, Inc., 1973.

Habermas, Jurgen. The Theory of Communicative Action, vol. I, II. Boston, MA: Beacon, 1984, 1987.

Mysticism and Religious Traditions. Edited by Stephen Katz. New York: Oxford University Press, 1983.

Niebuhr, H. Richard. The Meaning of Revelation. New York: Macmillan Publishing Co., 1941.

Roof, Wade Clark. Community and Commitment. New York: Elsevier, 1978.

Segal, Paul. Paul the Convert: the Apostalate and Apostasy of Saul the Pharisee. New Haven, CN: Yale University Press, 1987.

Troeltsch, Ernst. The Social Teaching of the Christian Churches, vol. I, II. Louisville, KY: Westminster/John Knox Press, 1992; original German edition published in 1912; first English translation published in 1931 by George Allen and Unwin Ltd., London and the Macmillan Co., NY.

      Wuthnow, Robert. <u>Communities of Discourse.</u> Cambridge, MA: Harvard University Press, 1989.

Index

Atonement, 149, 159, 160
Augustine, 73, 133
Baptism, 8, 128, 130, 131, 142, 172
Bellah, Robert, 39, 109, 165, 188
Beloved Community, 7, 27, 30, 31,
   33, 36, 75, 76, 79, 82, 83, 84, 85,
   86, 88, 92, 96, 98, 99, 108, 148,
   159, 163, 175, 176
Berger, Peter, 140, 188
Bond, 17, 18, 31, 47, 48, 61, 62, 119,
   122, 130, 137, 148, 164, 169, 171
Bonds, 7, 8, 12, 18, 36, 47, 48, 60,
   61, 81, 95, 110, 112, 118, 127,
   130, 137, 145, 156, 159, 162, 164,
   165, 167, 170, 171, 172
Bowker, John, 158, 188
Bridge, 8, 12, 16, 25, 26, 28, 29, 42,
   77, 114, 162, 164, 169, 170
Brown, Raymond, 35, 125
Buddhism, 147, 148, 172
Cady, Linnell E., 22, 92, 181
Change, 5, 8, 22, 23, 25, 28, 101,
   110, 116, 121, 124, 136, 141, 152,
   188
Church, 11, 18, 19, 32, 34, 35, 36,
   37, 43, 44, 45, 50, 51, 53, 55, 56,
   57, 58, 59, 60, 61, 63, 64, 65, 66,
   67, 68, 69, 70, 71, 72, 74, 75, 79,
   83, 88, 89, 96, 97, 98, 102, 109,
   119, 120, 121, 122, 123, 124, 125,
   127, 128, 129, 130, 132, 133, 134,
   135, 136, 137, 139, 147, 148, 150,
   159, 162, 171, 185, 186
Coherence, 22, 23, 24, 56, 78, 81,
   82, 86, 117, 118, 121, 125, 131,
   132, 134, 141, 142, 145, 155, 161,
   162
Common Church, 44
Communal religious consciousness,
   19, 49, 53, 61, 68, 131, 133
Communion, 8, 52, 136
Communities, 1, 3, 5, 6, 7, 8, 11, 17,
   30, 36, 37, 38, 43, 44, 47, 48, 49,
   50, 51, 52, 55, 64, 69, 74, 75, 76,
   80, 83, 84, 85, 87, 88, 90, 92, 97,
   98, 99, 102, 107, 108, 110, 114,
   116, 119, 120, 123, 135, 136, 138,
   139, 141, 142, 144, 145, 148, 153,
   159, 162, 163, 164, 165, 166, 167,
   169, 170, 171, 172, 174, 175, 176,
   177, 189
Communities of loyalty, 84, 85
Community, 1, 2, 5, 6, 7, 8, 9, 10,
   11, 12, 13, 15, 16, 17, 18, 20, 22,
   23, 24, 25, 26, 27, 28, 29, 30, 31,
   32, 33, 34, 35, 36, 37, 38, 39, 40,
   43, 44, 45, 46, 47, 48, 49, 50, 51,
   52, 53, 54, 55, 56, 57, 58, 59, 60,
   61, 62, 63, 64, 65, 66, 67, 68, 69,
   70, 71, 72, 73, 74, 75, 76, 77, 78,
   79, 80, 81, 82, 83, 84, 85, 86, 87,
   88, 89, 90, 91, 92, 93, 94, 95, 96,
   97, 98, 99, 101, 102, 103, 106,
   107, 108, 109, 110, 111, 112, 113,
   114, 115, 116, 117, 118, 119, 120,
   121, 122, 123, 124, 127, 128, 129,
   130, 131, 132, 133, 134, 135, 136,
   137, 138, 139, 140, 141, 142, 143,
   144, 145, 146, 148, 149, 150, 151,
   152, 153, 154, 155, 156, 157, 158,
   159, 160, 161, 162, 163, 164, 165,
   166, 167, 168, 169, 170, 171, 172,
   174, 175, 176, 177, 178, 180, 181,
   182, 188
Concept, 3, 4, 13, 49, 50, 61, 72, 73,
   175, 185
Conscience, 65, 104, 144
Consciousness, 1, 2, 8, 10, 11, 12,
   13, 16, 17, 18, 19, 20, 24, 25, 29,
   30, 34, 40, 43, 47, 48, 49, 50, 51,
   52, 53, 54, 55, 56, 57, 58, 59, 61,
   62, 63, 64, 65, 66, 67, 68, 69, 70,
   71, 72, 73, 74, 76, 77, 79, 81, 87,
   88, 89, 92, 93, 94, 95, 96, 98, 102,
   104, 106, 107, 108, 109, 111, 116,
   117, 118, 119, 120, 121, 122, 123,
   125, 127, 129, 130, 131, 132, 133,
   134, 135, 136, 137, 141, 142, 143,
   144, 145, 146, 147, 148, 149, 151,
   152, 155, 156, 157, 160, 161, 163,
   170, 171, 172, 187
Contextual, 33, 117

Contingency, 7, 13, 19, 22, 23, 24, 35, 117, 118, 119, 121, 131, 134, 135, 139, 155, 161, 166, 172
Contingent, 6, 7, 8, 15, 17, 22, 23, 24, 25, 30, 32, 33, 36, 41, 56, 60, 69, 70, 82, 86, 96, 105, 113, 118, 120, 121, 122, 131, 132, 133, 134, 135, 136, 137, 139, 141, 142, 143, 144, 146, 147, 149, 151, 152, 154, 159, 160, 161, 163, 164, 165, 166, 167, 168, 169, 171, 172
Corliss, Richard, 15, 186
Corrington, Robert, 114, 180
Culture, 1, 12, 17, 25, 39, 49, 104, 109, 135, 142, 165, 166, 170, 174, 175, 186
Customs, 40, 76, 78, 142, 148, 150, 153, 176
Descartes, Rene, 3
Division, 135, 174
Doctrine, 7, 8, 13, 17, 19, 28, 29, 32, 37, 54, 65, 66, 67, 68, 69, 75, 78, 79, 83, 86, 90, 96, 136, 144, 150, 155, 161, 162, 164, 166, 170, 175, 176, 177
Durkheim, Emile, 150, 188
Duty, 59, 101, 102, 176, 181
Ethics, 11, 16, 51, 57, 64, 65, 100, 139, 181, 183, 185
Evil, 5, 43, 82, 84, 86, 88, 105, 156, 158, 159
Experience, 1, 2, 3, 4, 5, 6, 8, 11, 13, 15, 19, 23, 25, 26, 32, 34, 40, 41, 42, 43, 45, 46, 47, 48, 49, 50, 51, 52, 53, 55, 56, 57, 66, 67, 69, 70, 71, 72, 73, 77, 78, 79, 80, 81, 82, 83, 87, 90, 92, 94, 95, 100, 102, 106, 109, 110, 111, 112, 113, 114, 115, 116, 117, 118, 126, 127, 139, 146, 148, 150, 152, 154, 157, 158, 159, 161, 162, 163, 164, 165, 167, 169, 170, 171, 172, 177, 186
Experience, religious, 1, 2, 3, 4, 5, 6, 11, 12, 13, 18, 22, 23, 24, 25, 31, 32, 40, 41, 42, 43, 45, 46, 47, 48, 49, 50, 51, 52, 56, 66, 68, 69, 78, 80, 81, 83, 90, 95, 109, 110, 111, 112, 113, 114, 117, 139, 146, 150, 161, 162, 163
Faith, 3, 4, 11, 13, 18, 19, 20, 30, 33, 37, 40, 48, 49, 50, 60, 66, 67, 69, 70, 72, 73, 80, 101, 107, 109, 116, 119, 120, 122, 124, 126, 128, 129, 133, 137, 183, 185, 186
Gadamer, Hans Georg, 15, 16, 188
Gemeingeist, 60, 73
Gemeinsinn, 60
Gimello, Robert, 111
God, 2, 3, 4, 18, 20, 32, 53, 55, 56, 57, 58, 59, 61, 63, 64, 65, 69, 70, 71, 72, 73, 74, 80, 86, 89, 90, 95, 96, 103, 107, 109, 110, 111, 116, 117, 118, 119, 120, 121, 122, 124, 125, 127, 130, 132, 133, 135, 144, 150, 156, 163, 171, 172
Good, 84, 103, 104, 105, 120, 156, 158, 159, 176
Grammatical interpretation, 10
Habermas, Jurgen, 123, 175, 188
Hermeneutics, 9, 10, 11, 12, 13, 14, 15, 16, 22, 183, 185, 187
Hick, John, 2, 5, 113
History, 8, 17, 27, 32, 36, 37, 40, 46, 56, 60, 65, 71, 77, 83, 86, 89, 90, 110, 121, 122, 127, 132, 134, 135, 139, 140, 141, 154, 159, 162, 164, 165, 166, 167, 185, 186
Hodgson, Peter, 60, 185
Holy Spirit, 59, 60, 61, 62, 63, 65, 69, 90, 121
Ideal, 2, 6, 7, 8, 11, 12, 13, 15, 16, 17, 19, 21, 24, 30, 33, 34, 35, 36, 37, 38, 39, 41, 42, 43, 46, 50, 54, 56, 66, 67, 75, 76, 79, 80, 82, 84, 85, 86, 87, 91, 93, 95, 96, 98, 100, 102, 103, 104, 105, 106, 110, 112, 113, 114, 120, 121, 122, 130, 134, 135, 136, 139, 140, 141, 142, 143, 144, 145, 146, 147, 148, 149, 150, 151, 153, 154, 155, 157, 159, 161, 162, 163, 164, 165, 166, 167, 168, 169, 170, 171, 172, 174, 176, 177
Imagination, 25, 26, 45
Inge, W. R., 1
Interconnectedness, 102

Interpretation, 1, 2, 5, 6, 8, 9, 10, 11,
12, 13, 14, 15, 17, 20, 22, 23, 25,
26, 27, 28, 29, 30, 31, 32, 33, 34,
35, 36, 38, 40, 43, 46, 47, 49, 51,
75, 77, 78, 80, 81, 86, 87, 90, 91,
94, 95, 96, 97, 99, 102, 108, 109,
110, 111, 112, 113, 114, 115, 117,
120, 123, 124, 125, 126, 127, 132,
137, 138, 139, 140, 141, 142, 143,
144, 145, 146, 147, 148, 149, 150,
151, 152, 153, 155, 156, 157, 158,
159, 160, 161, 162, 163, 164, 166,
167, 168, 169, 170, 171, 172, 176,
181, 185, 186, 188
James, William, 3, 4, 5, 30, 78, 79,
95, 146
Jesus, 11, 13, 18, 19, 20, 32, 33, 34,
35, 36, 37, 51, 53, 54, 55, 56, 57,
58, 59, 61, 63, 65, 67, 68, 69, 70,
71, 72, 73, 74, 78, 90, 96, 109,
117, 120, 121, 122, 123, 124, 125,
126, 127, 128, 130, 132, 133, 144,
149, 157, 167, 171, 172, 183, 185
Jones, Rufus, 2
Kant, Immanuel, 3, 4, 26
Katz, Stephen, 109, 188
Klemm, David, 16, 117, 185
Language, 1, 4, 6, 7, 9, 10, 11, 12,
15, 16, 17, 18, 25, 41, 43, 47, 48,
49, 50, 54, 64, 76, 78, 123, 135,
136, 141, 142, 162, 163, 166, 169,
170, 175, 177, 186
Lindbeck, George, 175
Locke, John, 137
Lord's Supper, 79, 128, 129, 130,
131, 142, 172
Love, 30, 42, 47, 73, 76, 82, 83, 84,
85, 89, 90, 97, 99, 102, 103, 107,
108, 109, 120, 142, 146, 147, 148,
150, 156, 157, 159, 176
Loyalty, 30, 32, 35, 36, 37, 38, 47,
62, 75, 76, 78, 80, 81, 82, 83, 84,
85, 86, 87, 88, 90, 93, 97, 98, 99,
100, 101, 102, 103, 104, 105, 106,
107, 108, 136, 142, 146, 150, 153,
156, 158, 159, 160, 172, 174, 176,
181
Martyrdom, 101, 102, 176

Meaning, 2, 4, 6, 7, 8, 10, 11, 12, 13,
14, 15, 16, 17, 19, 23, 24, 25, 26,
27, 28, 29, 31, 32, 33, 34, 35, 36,
38, 39, 42, 43, 44, 45, 46, 54, 60,
66, 68, 75, 77, 79, 80, 81, 82, 91,
93, 95, 97, 102, 106, 109, 110,
112, 114, 116, 119, 123, 125, 126,
129, 131, 137, 139, 141, 143, 144,
146, 149, 150, 152, 154, 155, 157,
158, 161, 162, 163, 164, 165, 166,
167, 168, 169, 170, 171, 172, 177,
188
Mediate, 6, 8, 34, 42, 50, 58, 60, 93,
112, 113, 128, 136, 148, 152, 155,
159, 163, 164, 165, 170, 171
Mediation, 29, 34, 55, 74, 112, 117,
121, 172
Metaphysical, 34, 90, 91, 92, 142
Moore, Walterj, 21
Mysticism, 1, 2, 5, 10, 112, 188
Natural Communities, 84, 85, 87,
108
Need, 3, 13, 18, 19, 20, 23, 28, 30,
36, 37, 47, 51, 53, 57, 58, 61, 63,
76, 80, 81, 82, 83, 84, 87, 89, 94,
97, 98, 99, 100, 101, 103, 105,
112, 117, 119, 134, 135, 137, 139,
140, 141, 149, 151, 152, 154, 157,
158, 164, 165, 166, 167, 169, 174,
175, 176
Niebuhr, R.R., 17
On Religion, 39, 40, 42, 44, 48, 69,
71, 183, 184
Oppenheimer, Frank, 29, 31, 76, 77,
91, 92, 93, 100, 141, 142, 152
Palmer, Richard, 14, 185
Pannenberg, Wolfhart, 18, 57, 185
Particular, 3, 6, 7, 8, 9, 10, 11, 13,
16, 17, 23, 24, 29, 32, 40, 41, 44,
45, 46, 48, 49, 50, 51, 54, 65, 67,
77, 80, 81, 85, 86, 87, 98, 102,
104, 105, 111, 116, 117, 118, 119,
120, 121, 134, 135, 136, 139, 140,
142, 144, 150, 152, 154, 158, 162,
163, 164, 165, 166, 169, 170, 171,
172, 174, 175, 176, 177
Patriotism, 47, 101, 102, 176

Paul, 25, 30, 32, 34, 36, 37, 38, 63, 79, 85, 97, 102, 109, 110, 111, 113, 139, 144, 145, 148, 156, 180, 188
Penner, Hans, 113
Perception, 23, 86, 110, 158, 162
Piety, 11, 51, 52, 55, 116, 117, 118
Prayer, 8, 122, 130, 131, 172
Preaching, 7, 8, 18, 19, 20, 58, 59, 60, 64, 70, 71, 122, 123, 126, 127, 131, 133, 170, 172
Proudfoot, Wayne, 112, 186
Reason, 3, 4, 5, 20, 25, 26, 55, 65, 67, 76, 80, 81, 86, 90, 95, 100, 108, 122, 124, 126, 139, 153, 154, 156, 165, 166
Redeker, Martin, 59, 185
Religious consciousness, 1, 11, 17, 18, 19, 20, 30, 40, 47, 48, 49, 50, 52, 53, 54, 55, 56, 57, 61, 62, 63, 64, 65, 66, 67, 68, 69, 70, 71, 72, 73, 79, 94, 95, 98, 116, 117, 119, 120, 123, 125, 129, 130, 131, 132, 133, 134, 135, 136, 137, 141, 142, 143, 145, 147, 148, 149, 151, 152, 155, 157, 161
Religious experience, 1, 2, 3, 4, 5, 6, 11, 12, 13, 18, 22, 23, 24, 25, 31, 32, 40, 41, 42, 43, 45, 46, 47, 48, 49, 50, 51, 52, 56, 66, 68, 69, 78, 80, 81, 83, 90, 95, 109, 110, 111, 112, 113, 114, 117, 139, 146, 150, 161, 162, 163
Ritual, 18, 44, 128, 162, 164
Royce, Josiah, 1, 2, 30, 34, 93, 94, 95, 106, 169, 178, 179, 180, 181, 182
Russell, Bertrand, 5
Sacraments, 44, 127, 128, 129, 130
Salvation, 6, 8, 24, 32, 33, 57, 79, 80, 81, 82, 83, 84, 89, 90, 94, 95, 97, 98, 99, 100, 101, 102, 103, 107, 108, 140, 141, 144, 146, 147, 148, 149, 151, 152, 154, 155, 157, 158, 159, 160, 164, 171, 172, 173
Schleiermacher, Friedrich, 1, 9, 12, 59, 66, 135, 184, 185, 186

Scripture, 7, 13, 65, 68, 69, 70, 71, 122, 124, 127, 129, 131, 170, 172
Segal, Alan, 111, 139
Sign, 7, 8, 31, 32, 33, 34, 35, 36, 37, 38, 41, 43, 44, 45, 46, 50, 52, 55, 56, 67, 86, 91, 92, 94, 96, 97, 99, 100, 103, 105, 107, 114, 122, 128, 129, 130, 139, 140, 141, 142, 143, 144, 148, 152, 166, 167, 169, 170, 171, 172, 181
Smith, John E., 31, 96, 181, 182
Social, 2, 8, 11, 26, 29, 30, 31, 34, 36, 39, 40, 43, 46, 47, 49, 51, 52, 54, 55, 56, 64, 75, 76, 78, 79, 80, 81, 83, 84, 86, 87, 88, 89, 90, 91, 92, 93, 94, 95, 96, 97, 99, 100, 101, 102, 103, 105, 106, 117, 139, 141, 142, 143, 144, 146, 148, 151, 156, 157, 159, 164, 165, 170, 175, 180, 181, 188
Sources of Religious Insight, 79, 80, 94, 106, 107, 146, 151, 153, 157, 178
Strauss, David, 37, 185
Suffering, 8, 82, 158, 171, 188
Swidler, Leonard, 113
Symbol, 7, 22, 34, 36, 54, 67, 71, 85, 90, 114, 129, 147, 175, 176, 177
Technical interpretation, 10
Teleological, 64, 142, 143, 145, 146
The Problem of Christianity, 29, 30, 31, 34, 36, 75, 76, 78, 79, 87, 88, 90, 91, 92, 95, 96, 97, 99, 100, 101, 102, 106, 107, 108, 140, 142, 143, 144, 147, 150, 153, 155, 159, 179
Time, 1, 3, 4, 12, 17, 24, 33, 36, 37, 46, 55, 60, 65, 67, 70, 73, 75, 88, 89, 91, 92, 108, 110, 118, 119, 121, 123, 125, 126, 129, 132, 133, 134, 135, 136, 137, 145, 152, 166, 176
Tradition, 7, 8, 12, 13, 17, 22, 28, 44, 49, 65, 69, 70, 71, 73, 77, 78, 79, 109, 111, 112, 113, 123, 136, 139, 141, 145, 147, 158, 161, 170
Trinity, 59, 60, 96
Troeltsch, Ernst, 2, 36, 72, 185, 188

Underhill, Evelyn, 2
Understanding, 2, 3, 5, 6, 8, 9, 10,
  11, 13, 14, 15, 16, 17, 18, 19, 23,
  25, 26, 27, 28, 29, 32, 35, 37, 39,
  40, 44, 45, 46, 47, 48, 49, 50, 51,
  52, 53, 57, 59, 62, 66, 67, 68, 71,
  76, 77, 82, 90, 91, 92, 93, 97, 105,
  109, 110, 111, 112, 114, 116, 117,
  119, 120, 121, 122, 123, 124, 126,
  127, 129, 130, 135, 140, 142, 143,
  148, 149, 151, 154, 155, 156, 158,
  165, 171, 186
Unity, 3, 15, 17, 24, 26, 28, 32, 35,
  60, 61, 77, 79, 81, 82, 83, 85, 87,
  89, 94, 96, 98, 99, 100, 101, 103,
  104, 106, 108, 109, 114, 119, 128,
  131, 132, 134, 135, 145, 146, 150,
  151, 155, 157, 159, 166, 170, 171
Universal, 3, 14, 22, 23, 27, 30, 32,
  33, 34, 36, 37, 38, 41, 42, 48, 49,
  56, 58, 62, 63, 65, 81, 82, 85, 86,
  88, 90, 91, 92, 94, 97, 99, 100,
  101, 104, 105, 107, 108, 113, 116,
  134, 135, 136, 140, 143, 146, 147,
  150, 152, 154, 155, 156, 160, 165,
  166, 170, 171
Value, 2, 4, 7, 27, 28, 33, 35, 36, 39,
  48, 66, 67, 70, 75, 91, 96, 107,
  111, 113, 140, 163, 165, 166, 177,
  182
Verheyden, Jack, 109, 183
Visible Church, 44, 83, 97, 133, 134,
  136
Will, 1, 4, 6, 7, 8, 16, 20, 24, 28, 29,
  33, 38, 45, 48, 58, 60, 62, 64, 65,
  68, 74, 75, 76, 78, 80, 81, 82, 83,
  88, 89, 92, 94, 95, 98, 99, 101,
  102, 103, 111, 113, 114, 115, 120,
  122, 130, 135, 138, 140, 144, 151,
  152, 153, 154, 157, 158, 160, 163,
  169, 172, 177
Wittgenstein, Ludwig, 10, 162
Worship, 33, 131
Wuthnow, Robert, 47, 88, 109, 141,
  175, 189